THE NEW HAMPSHIRE
DIVORCE
HANDBOOK

THE NEW HAMPSHIRE
DIVORCE
HANDBOOK

Second Edition

by

ATTORNEY
HONEY HASTINGS

Amoskeag
Press

Composed at Hobblebush Books, Brookline, NH (www.hobblebush.com)

Printed in the United States of America

Second Edition

PUBLISHERS CATALOGING-IN-PUBLICATION DATA:
(Provided by Quality Books, Inc.)

Hastings, Honey.
 The New Hampshire divorce handbook / Honey Hastings.
-- 2nd ed.
 p. cm.
 Includes bibliographical references and index.
 LCCN 2007904864
 ISBN-13: 978-1-893421-01-1
 ISBN-10: 1-893421-01-5

 1. Divorce--Law and legislation--New Hampshire--
Popular works.   I. Title.

 KFN1300.Z9H37 2007   346.74201'66
                             QBI07-600190

Several chapters first appeared in a column entitled "NH Law" in *Momentum*, the monthly publication of New Hampshire Mensa. Other chapters began as handouts prepared for and distributed to the author's clients. The "definitions" were first published on the author's web site, www.nhdivorce.com.

Amoskeag Press
P.O. Box 33, Temple, New Hampshire 03084
www.AmoskeagPress.com

Quantity discounts are available on bulk purchases.
For information please contact the publisher.

An important caution:

The material in this handbook is offered only as legal information. It is not legal advice. Anyone facing a divorce or other family law problem in New Hampshire needs legal advice. The same is true if you have questions about how New Hampshire law applies to your personal life. Legal advice is available only from a licensed New Hampshire lawyer to whom you have given the facts about your particular family situation. Chapter 5 of this book gives further information on finding, consulting, and hiring an appropriate New Hampshire lawyer for your problem or question.

The material on taxes is likewise general tax information and not tax advice. You will need to get tax advice from a qualified individual, such as a CPA or tax lawyer.

Also note that some of the information in this book may become outdated due to changes in the law. Family law, tax law, and the procedures for court cases change in some way every year. For updates, check www.NHDivorceHandbook.com.

acknowledgments

Many thanks to numerous colleagues who read chapters, generously shared their expertise, and offered encouragement, both for the first edition and the second. Members of the New Hampshire Bar Association who offered comments on this edition: John D. Cameron, Joshua L. Gordon, and Doreen F. O'Connor.

My special thanks to Timothy R. Hepburn, CPA, for updating the financial planning and tax chapters, to Attorney John Cameron for writing the foreword, and to Attorney Charlotte S. Guyer, who got me to write the first edition by repeatedly asking me when I was going to do it!

Paula Spear, my patient administrative assistant, handled all the publishing bureaucracy, typed the manuscript and saw it through many revisions. Sid Hall Jr., editor and book designer, turned my words into a real book to help New Hampshire families.

*To my clients, who have
taught me much about
the human capacity
to survive loss, to adapt,
and to grow*

*To everyone in New Hampshire
facing the difficulty of divorce,
with the hope they can
achieve a "good" divorce
and can cooperate in
co-parenting their children*

checklist finder

*Use this page as a quick reference to bulleted lists
and checklists found throughout the book.*

contents

1. The Basics of Family Law

2. Parenting During and After Divorce

3. Money and Divorce

4. How to Make Divorce Decisions

8. Going to Court

9. Domestic Violence

10. Parenting—The Law

15. Appeals

16. After Divorce

Appendix A • More Tax Tips 225

Appendix B • Standard Order of Paragraphs

Appendix C • Checklists and Resources

Definitions 271

Index 285

foreword to the first edition

NO ONE WANTS TO GET divorced. Everyone enters marriage with the expectation that it is for a lifetime, and that it will bring happiness. Plans are made. Children are born. A family comes to be. With all these expectations placed on marriage, it is no wonder that divorce is usually so painful. During a divorce we tend to focus on our emotions, our doubts about the past and our fears for the future. Yet, in the end, there is something else which ultimately determines how successful the divorce will be: the law, and how the parties involved approach the law.

That is where this handbook comes in. When a marriage ends, we are confronted with the reality of making new financial arrangements, resolving custody questions, and choosing the right process for resolving disputes. Attorney Honey Hastings' book brings two principles to this process, ones that are not always found together: her book is comprehensive, and it is written in plain English. By focusing clearly on the law, it will help families focus on the crucial decisions they need to make. Hopefully, it will make the divorce less painful.

Attorney Hastings is recognized as a leading expert on divorce law in New Hampshire. She was instrumental in the organization of the Family Law Section of the New Hampshire Bar Association, and she lectures regularly on family law. She began her private law practice in Nashua in 1982. Today she also manages a mediation practice.

Divorce decisions are difficult. The division of income and assets almost always leaves both parties with less than they had when they were married. This handbook carefully explains the ins and outs of child support, alimony, and property division. The inclusion of several chapters by CPA Hollis McGuire furnishes a comprehensive overview of financial planning, taxes, and other money issues. With a deeper knowledge of both divorce and tax law, the reader can better make critical financial decisions.

If there is one principle that professionals agree upon, it is that *conflict* between parents over the daunting issues of divorce is harmful to their children's development and emotional health. Parents do not set out to hurt their children. But a lack of understanding about how the divorce will affect the children, and how best to communicate during the divorce process, often result in choices that are not in the best interest of the children. Attorney Hastings pays close attention to this problem in an early chapter of this handbook, and gives parents the essential information they need to minimize conflict and make good decisions.

I would like to thank Attorney Hastings personally for devoting so much energy to writing this book. As a Professor of Family Law, I strive to teach new lawyers that the practice of family law requires more than knowledge. It also requires compassion and a desire to help people through crisis. I believe that the adversarial system is an appropriate and necessary way to resolve the intransigent problems of some divorcing families. However, the system which I believe works best for most families, and the one that is advocated by Attorney Hastings in this book, is one that *minimizes* conflict and looks to the individuals who are divorcing to fashion solutions that work for their own family.

Attorney Hastings brings the same compassionate and pragmatic approach to her practice that she recommends and describes in this book. Visiting this book is like visiting her office. The book is arranged (and cross-referenced) so that everyone will find what they need quickly and easily, saving days, perhaps months of research. Those facing a divorce can see clearly how the law will affect them, and even more importantly, how the keys to the resolution of their legal problems lie primarily in their own hands.

Ellen Musinsky
Professor of Family Law
Franklin Pierce Law Center
Concord, New Hampshire

foreword to the second edition

IN EARLY AMERICA divorce was rare. In the eighteenth and nineteenth centuries most couples remained together by a common bond: the efforts of both were very much needed for their individual and mutual survival. The marriage was further solidified by the law in those days: a wife's personal property belonged to her husband—if she left him, she took nothing. Even so, some early Americans sought divorces, but for most of those that did, property distribution and placement of children were clear "black and white" decisions.

Things began to change in the nineteenth century for both marriage and divorce law, as the divorce rate began a slow climb. In 1880 the divorce rate in the United States was about 5 percent—one in twenty marriages ended in divorce. Thirty years later it had risen to about 10 percent, and today it continues to hover around 50 percent.

While the divorce rate grew, the laws governing divorce also expanded dramatically. Today New Hampshire's divorce laws contain nuances and technicalities that are difficult for the layman to define or explain in readily objective terms. Rather, they are typically applied and interpreted by attorneys, or by judges and marital masters, and these judicial officers apply their "judicial discretion." More important, social research into the effects of divorce on children and especially the negative effect on children of parental conflict has led to major changes in the determination of parental rights and responsibilities when parents are divorcing or separating in New Hampshire.

This handbook has been carefully and thoughtfully revised by Attorney Hastings. In it she presents—with the same understanding and attention to detail of the first edition—a comprehensive view of the divorce process in New Hampshire, including the recent changes that have occurred in law in the state. She does so with the same practical, common-sense and plain-speak style as before.

This handbook provides, as no other source does, a thought-provoking look at the process of divorce. Additionally, it provides helpful information that enables the reader to make informed choices if confronted with divorce or separation: choices about the optimum process for resolving disputes; choices for resolving parental rights and responsibilities questions; choices for fairly and equitably dividing marital property; and choices that will optimize each spouse's ability to make critical financial decisions.

The handbook's chapters entitled "Parenting—The Law" and "Parenting During and After Divorce" are particularly important. Divorcing or separating parents are not just any two litigants brought to court by an accident or an alleged wrongdoing. They are individuals who have been, and will continue to be, in a relationship due to the children they share. The quality of that relationship, now being restructured due to the divorce (or separation), will have a deep and lasting impact on the emotional and psychological health of the children. Attorney Hastings pays close attention to these concerns and provides essential information to parents that can be used to minimize conflict and make sound parenting decisions.

Attorney Hastings has long been respected as an expert on divorce law in New Hampshire. She was a key participant on the Governor's Task Force on Family Law and drafted the Parental Rights and Responsibilities Act of 2005. She lectures regularly on family law, both to members of the New Hampshire Bar and to certified family mediators. She has taken a strong stand in favor of a less- or non-adversarial approach to family matters in the courts, such that today her practice includes mediation, collaborative law, and parenting coordination. Her handbook echoes her philosophy that *conflict* in family legal matters must be minimized and that divorcing individuals who are able to create their own solutions amicably will inevitably reap important benefits for themselves and their children.

As a family law attorney who has been involved in both the creation of New Hampshire's family court and the development of the Parental Rights and Responsibilities Act, and whose practice has also changed course to emphasize parental integrity and non-adversarial approaches to separation or divorce, I applaud Attorney Hastings for her tireless efforts in first writing, and now revising, this handbook. The book is arranged in a way so as to simply and clearly present all the important information anyone faced with divorce or separation should need to know about the process, the options, and how the law effects them, and how they themselves can control the resolution of their legal problems.

John Cameron, MBA, JD
Laconia, New Hampshire
Mediator and Collaborative Law Attorney
Parenting Coordinator

introduction

THIS HANDBOOK is a user's guide to divorce in New Hampshire. It provides basic information on the legal, psychological, and financial aspects of divorce. While there are many books available on these topics, this is the only one written for people who are getting divorced in New Hampshire. Divorce law and procedure are different in every state. Books based on California or Illinois or New York divorce law are simply inaccurate when applied to New Hampshire.

While the handbook is addressed primarily to people who are, or may be, involved in a divorce, it will also be helpful to many others. Mediators, therapists, clergy, paralegals, lawyers, court staff, accountants, financial planners, and educators will find insights into the components of divorce that are not part of their professional training and experience.

Changes in the law

Since this handbook was first published in 1999 there have been substantial changes in New Hampshire family law and the procedures for divorce. Thanks to the work of the Task Force on Family Law, "custody" was abolished and New Hampshire has adopted a public policy that children do best when they have frequent and regular contact with both parents. What was the "custody" chapter has been completely rewritten to explain this policy and the Parental Rights and Responsibilities Act.

Parents are to work out a parenting plan showing how they will share responsibilities for their child. Mediation, either private or court-referred, is now used by more couples to work out their parenting plan and the other divorce issues. Another respectful method of decision-making has blossomed since 1999: collaborative practice. Litigation is no longer the expected way to make divorce decisions. The chapter on decision-making options has been updated to reflect these changes.

The Family Division—for many years an experiment in two counties—is gradually expanding across the state. By focusing on only family cases the Family Division has developed procedures, assembled staff, and selected judicial officers who can best help families through difficult times.

Other changes will surely come and updates to this book will be published at least yearly on www.NHDivorceHandbook.com. Please check this web site for changes in the law or procedures which could impact your divorce.

How the book is organized

There are two themes in this handbook: how to protect your child or children during a divorce, and how to take care of yourself. The handbook chapters are arranged to help a person who is new to the topic of divorce take up these issues in a useful order. There are four main sections:

Chapters 1–4 introduce New Hampshire law and procedure, show how to help your child through divorce, and explain how to make decisions.

Chapters 5–8 tell how to choose and work with a lawyer and how to deal with court papers and procedures.

Chapters 9–14 describe various aspects of the law, including how it applies to parenting, support, property division, and taxes.

Chapters 15–16 deal with life after the divorce, including appeal procedures.

The back of the book includes a variety of useful material: definitions of terms, important sources of information, books for children and adults, names of community and support groups, and Internet sites.

Plain language

I have made every effort to write in plain English. When legal terms and technical words are first used in the handbook, they are explained. You can also find these words, as well as technical terms frequently used in court papers by judges and lawyers, in the "Definitions" section at the back of the book.

Honey Hastings, JD

the basics
of family
law

1

Chapter 1

The Basics of Family Law

IF YOU ARE READING THIS book, you or your spouse, or both of you, are already considering divorce. You are about to embark on a journey that will change your lives and your children's lives forever. Pain, anger, and guilt will accompany you on this journey. You and your spouse may lash out at each other. Your divorce may turn into a war.

It doesn't have to be so. In my experience, two factors have made the process worse than it needs to be for many families: (1) anger, pain, guilt, and other negative emotions, (2) lack of information about decision-making options, divorce law, and children's needs. Couples try to use the court system to deal with the pain that divorce causes, or to punish their spouses. Some spouses take rigid positions without understanding the negative results that may follow. Others act in ways that hurt their negotiating positions, because they don't know the law.

A spouse who needs alimony, for example, may fail to pursue it because she thinks it is unavailable in New Hampshire; or a spouse may give up rights to the other spouse's retirement benefits, not knowing what he is entitled to. A spouse may move out of the family home without taking the proper steps. Some couples pursue contested divorces, despite the harm to their children and to their bank accounts, because of emotions or lack of information.

Many people unintentionally hurt their children by involving them in the divorce.

With better information you can make better decisions, in spite of the enormous stress of your marriage or civil union coming to an end. You can learn how divorce works. You can choose to participate in making the decisions in your divorce. You can choose to master your anger and pain and work toward a fair settlement of the divorce issues. You can protect your child or children from the worst consequences of divorce. You can find ways to co-parent your children despite the problems you have had in the relationship and the ultimate decision to divorce.

Most couples facing divorce want to understand the process and their options. They want to maintain control of their own divorce. You can do this only when you understand the legal basics. If you choose to be informed and active in your case, and to make fairness your goal, your emotional wounds will heal. You will survive your divorce, and so will your children. You will have a "good" divorce.

What is in this book?

The remainder of this chapter is an overview of New Hampshire divorce procedure and law. The following chapters provide in-depth discussion of specific topics, such as parenting, child support, alimony, and property division. At the back of the book, there are book lists, definitions of technical terms, web site lists, and other useful resources and information.

This book also covers three topics that a person facing divorce needs to know about:

- *How to parent your child through your divorce:*
  How you handle your divorce will make a
  considerable difference to your child. Chapter 2

contains much of what I have learned from child psychologists.

- *The five ways of making decisions in your divorce:* Choosing the method for making the decisions in your divorce is the most important decision and the first one to make. There are healthy decision-making options, alternatives to simply giving in to whatever your spouse wants, or engaging in World War III. Chapter 4 discusses all five options.

- *How to find the right lawyer for you and for your case:* Due to the stress and the emotional difficulty of divorce, many people do not make the best decisions about lawyers. They either hire the first lawyer they meet or they refuse to talk to a lawyer at all. Chapter 5 explains how to find the right lawyer for the legal services you need and chapter 6 tells how to make the most of the money you spend on legal fees.

Some basic legal terms

Divorce is a legal procedure to end a marriage or civil union. The Family Division of the Judicial Branch handles divorces. Each year, New Hampshire's vital statistics agency records over 5,000 divorces. It usually takes at least three or four months to get a divorce in New Hampshire; the average is seven months. In some cases, it can take three years or more.

If one spouse insists on getting a divorce, it is very difficult for the other to stop it. You don't need your spouse's permission to get a divorce. However, if you and your spouse agree on getting a divorce, you will save time and money.

Some people consider getting a *legal separation*, instead of a divorce (sometimes because of religious principles). This is a legal procedure to allow spouses to live apart permanently under court orders. Simply living apart is not the same as a legal separation. However, very few New Hampshire couples actually obtain a legal separation: there are approximately fifty each year. A married or "unionized" couple may choose to live apart without getting a legal separation or taking any other legal action.

The court paperwork and process for a legal separation is similar to a divorce. Assets are divided and support and parenting orders are made, just as in a divorce. In New Hampshire, legal separation is not a quick or simple procedure. It is a distinct legal process, which takes as long as a divorce, and costs as much. The marriage (or union) itself is not dissolved, the spouses are not free to remarry, and the wife may not resume her former name. With these exceptions, the material in this handbook also applies to legal separation.

An *annulment* is a legal procedure that is rarely used (about five per year), and only when there was some legal defect from the beginning of the marriage (or union). The annulment order declares that the marriage never existed. Because it is often difficult to prove the legal defect, an annulment generally takes longer and costs more than an uncontested divorce. (Note that this refers to a civil annulment. The annulment procedure in the Catholic Church is not a matter for the courts. See the resources section in appendix C for information on Catholic annulments.)

Parenting and child support disputes between parents that have never married are resolved in the same way as in a divorce case. The same law applies and the procedures are the same. If you are facing an "unwed" dispute, the chapters on parenting, support, and decision-making options will apply to your case. Alimony and property division laws do not apply to couples who were never married. All the divorce laws also apply to civil unions. In this book, the term "spouses" is used for both marriages and civil unions.

No-fault or fault?

In New Hampshire, the legal basis for a divorce may be either *no-fault* or *fault*. A *no-fault* divorce is based on "irreconcilable differences" which have caused the "irremediable breakdown" of the marriage or civil union. This means that the legal relationship has so broken down that one or both spouses are unwilling to continue it.

Examples of grounds for a *fault* divorce are: adultery, extreme cruelty, and endangering health and reason. Examples of rarely used grounds would be abandonment for two years, or joining the Shakers. Approximately 1 percent of New Hampshire divorces are granted on fault grounds. Some divorces are filed on fault grounds, but later the couple agrees to a no-fault divorce. (See chapter 13 for the impact of a fault divorce on property division.) In my experience, fault divorces are more expensive, take longer, and make co-parenting more difficult.

What are the issues in a divorce?

People rarely fight in court about whether or not there will be a divorce, because the court virtually always grants it. If divorcing spouses disagree, it is usually about one or more of the following legal issues:

- Parental rights and responsibilities (parenting)
- Child support
- Alimony
- Asset and debt division

This book discusses each of these topics in detail.

How do these issues get resolved?

There are five ways of resolving disputed divorce and parenting issues:

- Informal discussion between the spouses
- Mediation with a trained, impartial person
- Collaborative practice with trained lawyers
- Negotiation by lawyers
- A decision by the court, after a contested hearing

Because the terms of the divorce orders may affect the family for many years, it is wise for the couple to come to an agreement by themselves, or with the help of a mediator, or through their lawyers, before the final hearing. Most couples can make some, but not all, decisions by themselves. After all, many couples divorce because of their inability to communicate. Mediation and collaborative practice are decision-making choices that can improve communication. Mediation works well for many couples, and may be ordered by the court. Collaborative practice suits others who wish both to make their own decisions and to have the active involvement of their lawyers.

Negotiation through lawyers is the route traditionally chosen by couples. Most people work out, through their lawyers, the written agreements that become the basis of the divorce. Approximately 10 percent of divorce cases are decided by the court after a contested hearing. (See chapter 4 for more details on making decisions.)

What about "custody?"

New Hampshire has abolished the concept of "custody" in divorce. Instead, the parental rights and responsibilities of both parents are spelled out in a *parenting plan.* One aspect of this is the decision-making responsibilities for the child, including educational, medical, and religious decisions. After a divorce, or an unwed parenting case, most parents continue to have joint legal decision-making responsibilities.

Another part of the parenting plan is the *parenting schedule,* spelling out when each parent will have responsibility for the child or children. If the court decides the parenting schedule, the test is what is in the "best interest" of the child. There is no preference for mothers or fathers. Most parents work out the parenting plan, including the schedule. In recent years, more and more families have chosen parenting schedules that share the children on a 50/50 basis, or close to that. (See chapter 10 for details on parenting.)

How is child support determined?

Generally, one parent pays support (with rare exceptions), and may have to maintain life and health insurance. Child support is based on a complicated formula called the *Guidelines.* To get a *rough* idea of what that support will be, use this method: take the gross (all) of the supporting parent's income, subtract taxes and the cost of the health insurance covering the child, then apply to that figure the following percentages to estimate the amount of support:

- One child: 25 percent of net income
- Two children: 33 percent of net income
- Three children: 40 percent of net income
- Four or more children: 45 percent of net income

This is a simplified method for estimating child support! You must use the official forms and charts to set the accurate amount. (See chapter 11 on "Child Support" for more specifics, including when the Guidelines may not apply.)

Alimony, property division, and taxes

Alimony, or spousal support, can be awarded if one spouse needs it and the other spouse has the ability to pay it. A husband can receive alimony if he needs it and his wife is able to pay. The main characteristic of an alimony case is a substantial income difference between the spouses. (See chapter 12 for specific information on alimony.)

Unless the couple can reach an agreement, the court will divide the property (assets) in a fair and equitable way. This could mean a 50/50 division, or some other ratio. The assets to be divided include his assets, her assets, and joint assets. In doing so, the court may consider, among other things:

- The relative incomes of the spouses
- Each spouse's contribution as homemaker or wage earner
- The health of each spouse
- The total amount of family property
- The length of the marriage or union
- Fault (adultery, extreme cruelty, etc.)

See chapter 13 for more on property division.

Federal tax law can potentially lead to unexpected results in property division. A division initially intended to be 50/50 could become substantially unequal. It is important to consider taxes at the time of divorce to avoid an unanticipated tax bill. Tax exemptions and filing status are other tax issues. It is wise to have an accountant review the property division and other financial aspects of your divorce.

(Chapter 3 has basic information on financial planning, and chapter 14 and appendix A discuss taxes.)

What should I do (and not do) when first thinking about divorce?

Get advice (including legal and therapeutic) before you take any significant step. Gather information on your divorce options, and your family finances. Take time to assemble this information, review it thoughtfully, and make good decisions. Most importantly:

- Choose a respectful method of making decisions.
- Don't expose your child to hostility between you and your spouse.
- Don't reach an agreement with your spouse until you get legal advice.
- Don't make threats (except that you will see a lawyer).
- Don't let any argument deteriorate into violence (not even throwing a plastic cup).
- Don't move out without getting legal advice.
- Don't cancel insurance policies or change beneficiaries.
- Don't attempt to hide assets.
- Read chapters 2 and 4 of this book.

∞

parenting
during
and after
divorce

2

Chapter 2

Parenting During and After Divorce

Y OU MAY NOT EXPECT A book written by a lawyer to have a chapter on parenting. There are two reasons for me to include this chapter. First, a personal one: I am a child of divorce. Second, a professional one: In my years as a divorce lawyer and mediator, I have worked with, listened to, and read articles by child psychologists, therapists, and parent educators. Based on my experience with parents involved in divorce, I have become increasingly concerned about the impact on children of their parents' anger and bitterness.

The mental health professionals agree: it is not *divorce* that harms children; it is the *hostility* between their parents and how this is expressed. (Divorce may even be beneficial in some families.) You can prevent or minimize the harm to your child by what you say about the divorce and about the other parent, and by choosing a constructive method for making divorce decisions. Then work together to raise your child.

What shall I say to my child about the divorce?

Mental health professionals agree there are several things a child needs to hear:

- Both parents love the child.
- The child is *not* to blame for the divorce and cannot prevent it.
- The child will continue to see *both* parents (if this is the case).

- Both parents will continue to care for the child
  (if this is the case).

Saying these things once is not enough! You will need to give your child these messages repeatedly as he or she comes to terms with the divorce, and your actions must convey the same messages.

The best procedure is for both parents *together* to tell the child or children about the divorce, but they must put aside their hostility long enough to do so. Having everyone together is a little like a politician's press conference: everyone gets the same information at the same time. Gather the family together, explain the divorce and reassure your child or children about the points listed above.

You must be careful about how much you let your child know about the divorce. If either you or your spouse put your child "in the middle," the result may be serious psychological harm to your child. If the child has a therapist or counselor, ask that professional about what to say and not to say, and how to keep the child out of the middle. If the child doesn't have a therapist, your therapist can advise on these points. Or you may want to consult a child psychologist about the best way to help your child.

If you want to learn more about what parents should tell a child during divorce, read a book or two on helping children through divorce. (See "Books for Adults and Children" in appendix C of this book.) Sign up for a program on the impact of divorce on children. The Judicial Branch requires attendance at a "child impact program," and your taking it earlier in the process will benefit the children.

How can I help my child deal with the divorce?

Let go of your anger about what your spouse did or didn't do. This usually requires counseling from a qualified therapist. (But see the warning at the end of chapter 6.) Work with and not against the other parent in the care and upbringing of your children. If the co-parenting relationship has deteriorated due to the problems of the marriage or the stress of the divorce, consider counseling on co-parenting. This is different than marriage counseling, as the goal of co-parenting counseling is for divorced parents to work together in caring for, and nurturing the child.

If the other parent is unwilling to go to counseling with you, there are still things you can do:

- Get counseling yourself.
- Read books on children and divorce. (See the book list in the back of this book.)
- Attend a class or seminar on "parenting during (or after) divorce."

Take care of yourself, so you can take care of your child. Most important, don't expose your child to the anger between you and your spouse. As your child loves and needs both parents, such hostility is very harmful. As difficult as it may be to remain silent, negative statements about the other parent are always harmful to your child. Work on developing a business-like relationship with the other parent. Use the term "my child's mom" or "my child's dad," rather than "my ex-spouse."

Continue parenting your child. Parenting means providing care with consistency and predictability. Parenting means being there, to hold or comfort, to listen, to answer questions, to reassure, to set limits and boundaries. For babies and young children, care means hands-on care (diapering, bathing, feeding, putting to bed, getting up in the night), seeing to the child's medical care, and arranging for good day care (if needed).

For children ages seven to eleven, parenting includes preparing meals and eating together, going to the doctor, helping with school work, meeting regularly with teachers. For older children, most of the factors for children ages seven to eleven apply, but sharing activities and common interests and guiding the child toward adulthood are increasingly important. Examples are sports, hobbies, going places together, and planning for college.

What steps should I take to help my child through the divorce?

Be an active parent. Take care of your child and be involved in his or her life. Consider your priorities in allotting time to family, work, and other activities. Your child needs your time and attention more than he or she needs expensive outings or gifts. Sharing an ordinary day at home, doing the laundry, going shopping, preparing supper and doing the dishes, is quality time. Other good activities to share are bike rides, hikes, neighborhood walks, board games, and reading aloud.

Take your child to the doctor, stay home with your child when he or she is sick, assist with a school outing. If the other parent has a class, therapy session, or lawyer's appointment, offer to take care of the child.

It is important to attend the child's school and sports events, even if they occur during the other parent's time. But take care not to have hostility between you and the other parent spoil the event for the child.

My child is upset about leaving me to be with the other parent. How can I help?

Moving between parents can be stressful to your child. According to the mental health experts, this is why children resist the move, and cry or act out. Some parents reduce stress by scheduling transitions to occur during school or day care. That is, one parent delivers the child to school or day care, and the other parent picks up.

By having a regular routine that is followed each time your child returns to your care, the transition will be easier. If your child continues to have difficulties with transitions, get professional help.

A predictable transition routine is important. This can reassure your child that his or her relationship with you (and the other parent) is secure. For most children, the return to your home begins with processing the physical sensations, the look and smell of the place. Thus your child may need time alone at your house to adjust to the transition.

Divorce inevitably means change for your child. Try to maintain consistency in your parenting, so the child can rely on seeing you (and the other parent) at predictable times. Some old family rituals may fit your new life; by all means, continue them. Establish new customs that you as a single parent share with your child.

Is it important to keep the other parent informed?

Both during and after the divorce, most parents share decision-making. An important part of this is keeping the other parent informed about changes and events in the child's life. Even if you have sole decision-making responsibility, providing information to the other parent is generally in the child's interest. (See chapter 10 on "Parenting" for an explanation of New Hampshire law on this important topic.)

Often, in the midst of a divorce, the parents are unable to talk civilly to one another. One way around this is a weekly (or alternate week) e-mail, letter, memo, or newsletter to the other parent about the child. Two essentials: keep it factual and non-emotional, and do not have the child deliver the communication.

The communication could include the following, as applicable:

- Eating, sleeping, changes in toilet use
- Child's health update (illnesses, medication, appointments, injuries, test results)
- Behavior changes
- Play and friends
- Progress in school (projects, test scores, and report cards)
- Child's special events (plays, games, recitals)
- Parent-teacher events
- Child's doctor or therapist appointments
- Any need to vary parenting periods or pick-up arrangements

Keep communication about your child separate from communication about other issues, such as support, property division, and reviews of past offenses.

Why should I encourage my child's contact with the other parent?

You should support the child's relationship with the other parent and encourage regular contact. There are several reasons for this:

- The child loves and needs the other parent. This is so, no matter what you see as his or her deficits as a spouse (or even as a parent).
- The two of you will have to co-parent your child, at least through age eighteen.

- Interference with the other parent's parenting rights may justify the court changing the parenting plan.

How can I encourage my child's contact with the other parent?

- See that your child is ready for the exchange. Have the child's clothing and supplies packed on time. (Enclosing a list of items sent may encourage their return.)
- Allow the child to keep some clothing and personal items in the other parent's home.
- Speak positively about the child's time with the other parent.
- Be open to additional unscheduled time with the other parent if the other parent requests it or the child appears to need it.
- Be flexible about parenting periods. Offer "trades," or an extra hour added to a schedule time, as appropriate.
- Encourage the child to call the other parent and to talk when the other parent calls. Give the child privacy for these calls.
- Support the child's relationship with the other parent.
- Welcome the child's positive statements about his or her time with the other parent.
- If the child has an event that conflicts with the regular parenting schedule, encourage the child to work it out with the other parent.
- Maintain contact with your former spouse's parents and encourage your child to do so. This can mean phone calls, visits, or sending photos

and the child's drawings to distant grandparents.
If you had a good relationship with your in-laws
before the divorce, try to maintain or renew it.

Will my dating impact my child?

If you are dating during the divorce, be discreet. Generally, it is not in a child's interest to know about a dating relationship. It is too confusing to a child dealing with the losses of divorce. If your new relationship stands the test of time, you can introduce the child to your friend after the divorce. (Several books listed in appendix C have more to say about this sensitive topic.)

money
and
divorce

3

Chapter 3

Money and Divorce
by Hollis McGuire, MBA, CPA
(Updated by Timothy R. Hepburn, CPA, MBA)

Planning for your financial future

IF YOU EXPECT A FAIR financial outcome to your divorce, one that you can live with now and in the future, you must spend the time and energy to learn about taxes and other financial factors that will impact your divorce. By understanding the financial issues, you will be prepared to make divorce-related decisions on money and assets. These decisions can tremendously affect the future of your family.

This chapter is an overview of financial planning during divorce. Its goal is to increase your comfort level in thinking about and understanding this important topic. It is not meant to cover every situation. Financial planning and tax planning are interwoven and should be considered together when determining your future. You should consult a lawyer or an accountant (or both) for specific advice tailored to your needs. Chapter 14 covers tax basics, and other tax material may be found in appendix A.

How do I start to plan for cash flow after we separate?

Separating one household into two has an immediate financial impact on cash needs. It is more expensive to maintain two households. Standards of living will have to go down, unless the family's income increases or there was extra money prior to the separation.

Often, couples who separate cannot afford to support two households. Because of this, some couples choose to remain in the same house for the short term, or one adult may move in with other family members or to a house or apartment-sharing situation. You and your spouse may choose one of these options, or you may choose to reduce or eliminate certain expenses.

It is important to understand each spouse's cash flow needs when making these temporary decisions. If you make temporary decisions without considering the budgets needed for two households, the decisions could be unfair to you, to your spouse, or to both. (See chapter 4 for help on how to make these decisions.)

As part of your divorce paperwork, you must gather detailed information about your cash flow (income and expenses). To track past or ongoing expenses, consider using software such as Quicken. To organize this information or to estimate future needs, you can use the expense page of the court form called the *financial affidavit.* (available at the Self-Help Center on court web site: **www.courts.state.nh.us/**) This form divides expenses into categories (such as housing) and into specific expenses. For example, the insurance category includes homeowner's, renter's, medical, dental, vehicle, and life insurance.

You can use the financial affidavit expense categories as a worksheet to assist you in understanding your cash flow. Determining an amount for each type of expense and seeing the resulting total will prepare you to discuss your cash flow needs. Later you will have to complete the form, sign it under oath, and file it with the court. (See chapter 7 on "Court Papers" for more information on the financial affidavit.)

How much money will I need for day-to-day expenses?

The basic categories for your short-term cash needs are housing (including utilities, maintenance costs, and property taxes), insurance, health care costs, transportation, general and personal expenses (including food, clothing, and miscellaneous), child-related expenses (including costs for parenting time), financial expenses (including debt payments, federal and state income taxes, savings, retirement plans, IRAs, etc.). Give each of these items a target amount; then it will be easier to see if you can manage within any proposed agreement. Careful consideration of your current and projected expenses when filling in your financial affidavit will provide you with the information needed for planning. If a specific expense is an estimate, note this on the form.

During cash flow planning, remember to include expenses (such as insurance) that have been family expenses but will become your individual expense. Auto insurance will need to be changed from family to individual. Health insurance often needs to be purchased and paid for separately following the divorce. Coverage can continue for only a limited period through a spouse's employer (thirty-six months under the federal law called COBRA or New Hampshire law.) Depending on the state of employment or the state of residency, or both, there may be an additional charge. Get the figures for these costs from your insurance company, employer, or your spouse's employer.

You may wonder what you need to live separately. Most people in New Hampshire require $3,000–$7,000 per month cash flow after tax, for a one or two person family. Although you may not fall into this range, you can use this as a starting point when looking at your monthly cash flow needs. Obviously, some families live on less, usually by sharing expenses or receiving government assistance.

What are the dangers of credit cards and joint credit?

One financial pitfall is to rely too heavily on credit cards during the transition period to two households. Using a card to purchase everything from food to gasoline may result in your being unable to pay down the balance regularly.

Joint credit cards are also dangerous, as both partners are liable for any charges either one makes. Joint accounts should be canceled or frozen by both partners, unless your lawyer advises otherwise. Some divorcing spouses cut up both cards, but this does not close the account, and either spouse may ask the issuing bank to send a new card. Any joint debt or line of credit (such as a home equity account) remains a joint responsibility, even if there is an agreement or order that one spouse will pay.

What about our mortgage?

Mortgages are an important example of joint debt. They usually involve substantial sums due over many years. Even if one spouse receives the house and is to pay the mortgage, the other spouse is still responsible for the joint mortgage. Only refinancing the mortgage or paying off the mortgage ends this joint liability. Nothing that can be written into the divorce papers can change this. Signing a deed to transfer ownership does not affect the mortgage.

A joint mortgage liability also ties up the credit of the person no longer living in the house. Unless the joint mortgage balance is low, or the person's income is high, the joint mortgage may prevent the purchase of a new home.

What long-term cash requirements should be considered?

Long-term cash needs include retirement savings, as well as cash for personal goals, such as education for you and your children, or home purchase and improvement. Retirement planning should be considered a priority in any divorce agreement. This often makes the difference in later years between comfort and subsistence living. (Also see chapter 13 on "Property Division.")

Should I trade off the retirement plan for the house?

For most divorcing couples, the most valuable items of property are the house and all of the retirement plans. It is important to find out the current values of these assets and to think about the practical results of various ways of dividing them. (See chapter 13 on "Property Division.") Note that federal law allows retirement plans to be divided in a divorce without either taxes or penalties. A specific order called a *Qualified Domestic Relations Order* or QDRO (pronounced "quad-row") is needed for most plans.

Some couples consider having the wife get the house and the husband get all of the retirement plans. Although this may appear to be fair and practical in the short term, in the long term it may be unfair or impractical, or both. Before you agree to take the house (and give up a share of a retirement plan) stop, think, consider, and calculate! Can you afford to stay in this home long-term? For many people facing divorce, selling a large home and replacing it with more affordable housing will result in more financial stability and freedom in the future.

Consider also whether the house and retirement plan are of similar value. Retirement plans are often more valuable than the mortgaged house. If both spouses have retirement plans of similar value, usually each keeps his or her own. However, if one spouse has all or most of the retirement savings, then dividing the plans may be the fair solution. Avoiding taxes and penalties when dividing retirement benefits is discussed in chapter 14.

What factors should be considered in dividing retirement plans?

There are a number of types of retirement plans; take care that all plans have been considered. The statements for some retirement plans, such as 401(k)s and save plans, will show the current market value. The statements for most pensions only estimate the monthly benefit expected at the time of retirement. (A few provide the current value.)

Thus a pension, also known as a defined benefit plan, must usually be appraised for you to have an accurate idea of its value. It is critical that you have this information before you try to make a decision about a fair property settlement. There are some companies who will calculate the present value of a defined benefit plan for less than $400. These companies use the information supplied about the plan and their own computer formulas to produce a value. If you decide to use this method, it is essential that you provide them with sufficient and accurate information.

Use of a QDRO will not allow for a current distribution of defined benefit plan (pension) assets; the assets remain in a retirement account until the age is reached where distribution can be done without penalty. Many employers' defined contribution plans, such as 401(k)s, allow distributions under QDROs to be rolled into an Individual Retirement Plan (IRA), or other qualified plan, tax-free. Dividing

IRAs does not require a QDRO. IRAs can be divided in the divorce agreement or order. (See chapter 13 on "Property Division" and chapter 14 on "Taxes and Divorce" for more on retirement plans and QDROs.)

Can I get part of my spouse's Social Security?

If you were married for at least ten years, you could be entitled to a Social Security benefit based on your former spouse's earnings. Take into account, however, that your earnings, or, if remarried, your current spouse's earnings might result in a larger benefit to you. In addition, if the other parent becomes disabled, retires, or dies while your child is a minor, the child may be entitled to Social Security benefits. Contact the Social Security Administration to get information on what could happen in your case. (As Social Security is controlled by Federal law, nothing in the divorce agreement can change an entitlement.)

What about the family business?

Any business ownership creates a valuation issue at the time of divorce. If it is a very small business, which essentially creates a job only for the owner, then the valuation issues will be quite minimal, as there is no value or little value beyond the stream of income equivalent to a salary. Whether or not a business will require a formal valuation should be discussed with your CPA or attorney.

Most businesses should be valued formally by a professional who is specifically trained in valuation. The American Institute of Certified Public Accountants offers an accreditation in business valuation, which is designated as ABV (Accredited in Business Valuation). Professionals must have experience and pass an examination to be awarded the ABV designation. However, CPAs who have acquired the ABV are not the only professionals who are experienced or knowledgeable in valuation. Discuss with your lawyer or accountant your other options in choosing a valuation firm. It is important, whatever background the valuer has, that he or she be an independent, neutral person with no connection to the business being valued. The company's own CPA is unlikely to be neutral.

Valuation can be calculated in several different ways, including:

- An income approach
- A market approach
- An asset-based approach
- A cost approach

The person doing the valuation will use a number of techniques to come up with a balanced and equitable result. As a purchaser of valuation services, you will want to discuss the educational background of the valuation professional, the methods to be used, and his or her experience.

Does everything we own have to be valued?

Some items may appear to be "too much bother" to value. However, at a minimum, discuss the values of both intangible and tangible items with your lawyer and accountant. Remember, the current value, not the purchase price, is the most important figure. You may be surprised at how value builds over time, and it may be prudent to have items professionally appraised or valued. Significant items that are often overlooked include employee stock options, royalty payments, patents, and collections of any type, such as oriental rugs, guns, dolls, and so on.

What other steps should I take to put my finances in order?

Be careful to review your official financial documents as part of the divorce process. Use the checklist in appendix C of this book. Many people discover years later that, to their dismay, they have neglected to remove their former spouse from important financial documents as a co-owner or beneficiary. Consider insurance policies, annuities, and all other financial documents.

Financial planning is an essential part of the divorce process. Despite the emotional turmoil typical of divorce, you must gather information on cash flow and assets, get advice on your options, and take the time to make good decisions for your future.

Civil Unions and Money

Divorcing following a civil union presents unique financial needs as taxes and retirement benefits are governed by federal law. Federal law does not recognize civil unions. Consult a lawyer and a CPA knowledgeable about creative and fair solutions.

how to make divorce decisions

4

Chapter 4

How to Make Divorce Decisions

DIVORCE IS A TIME OF radical change, when many choices must be made. The decisions you make and the way you come to these decisions will change your life, your child's life, and your spouse's life. It is essential to get the information and the support you will need to make these decisions in the most constructive way.

Decisions about divorce may include the following significant issues: *parental rights and responsibilities, child support, alimony, division of assets and debts.* (Chapter 1 of this handbook contains a general discussion of these issues, and chapters 10 to 19 give details on specific issues.)

The most important divorce decision is choosing the method for making all the others. Decisions in divorce are made in one or more of the following ways:

- By the divorcing couple, *informally*, without professional help
- By the divorcing couple with the help of a *trained mediator*
- By the divorcing couple with the help of their *trained collaborative practice lawyers*
- By the divorcing couple, through *negotiation* by their lawyers
- By the master or judge, after a *contested hearing*

Whatever path to agreement is chosen, *a divorce agreement must be filed with the court* to be enforceable. This also applies to the parenting plan, if you have minor children. Whether you and your spouse make an agreement informally, through mediation, or with the help of lawyers, your agreement must be put into writing, signed by both of you and filed with the court. After a judge signs it, the agreement becomes a court order. If the master or judge makes the decisions, you will receive these decisions in the form of written orders.

What if I am afraid of my spouse?

In choosing the method or methods for making the decisions in your divorce, *consider your relationship with your spouse.* The informal method, mediation, and collaborative practice will work only if each spouse is able to speak freely about his or her needs. If you think you may be unduly pressured, hit, or beaten, you will not be able to work out a fair agreement on divorce issues. If there has been domestic violence (discussed in chapter 9) or some form of intimidation, it may be best to work out the agreement by negotiation through a lawyer. Do not give up on hiring a lawyer because you feel you cannot afford one. (See the "Resources" section in the back of this book for organizations that can help you.) If you are afraid of your spouse, it is important to get some counseling about domestic violence and your relationship. Your counselor may help you choose an appropriate decision-making method. (See chapter 9 on domestic violence for more information.)

What can I do to minimize the likelihood of a contested divorce?

Sometimes one or both spouses decide *not* to make the decisions for the family. Instead of using one or more of the methods (discussed in this chapter) of reaching agreement, they leave the decisions to a stranger: the master or judge. Often, emotional factors such as anger, pain, stubbornness, or the desire to punish the other spouse, enter into this choice.

Rationally and financially, however, agreement is almost always better. For your child, agreement is *always* best. Your child loves both parents and a contested hearing and the hostility that goes with it will hurt him or her.

What can you do to avoid your family getting caught in the adversarial trap (fighting in court)?

- Get counseling to understand why your marriage broke down, and your role in it (but see the caution on confidentiality at the end of chapter 6).

- Assure your child of your respect for the other parent's past and future role in the child's life.

- Avoid one-sided actions that will anger your spouse, unless there is a serious risk of harm.

- If there is someone else in your life, put the relationship on hold (or, at least, be discreet).

- Get assistance from professionals who support your goal to reach an agreement.

- Do not rush to file for divorce, unless you have a good reason. Often it is better to first make decisions, then file.

- If your lawyer suggests that you could "get more" or "do better" if you have a contested hearing, consider the risks and the alternatives. You can choose to compromise, instead of having the court decide.

- Consider the financial and emotional costs of a contested hearing. Ask your lawyer if it is possible that your spouse would "get more" or "do better."

To file or not to file, that is the question

Generally, you will decide to file for divorce promptly if you need the court's protection or help right away. For example:

- If you are a domestic violence victim.
- The other parent is denying you time with your child or may leave New Hampshire or the United States to do so.
- You are financially dependent on your spouse and he or she fails to support you.
- Your child lives primarily with you but the other parent refuses to provide support.
- Your spouse is likely to hide, sell, or give away assets.

If any of these factors apply, get legal advice promptly! Filing now may be essential.

But, if none of these factors apply, consider using the 21st century style—first, work out the agreement, then file for divorce. If you have been living apart for three months or more, you and your spouse probably have worked out temporary arrangements for money and the child or children. There may be no reason to file immediately. It may be better for your family to agree first, then file for divorce.

What are the advantages of agreeing first, then filing?

- Avoid unnecessary court events.

- Minimize bureaucratic paperwork.
- Reduce pressure to settle quickly.
- Use your lawyers' time constructively and efficiently.
  - A hasty filing may push your spouse to accelerate disputes.

Going to court, even for preliminary matters, is stressful. It does nothing to encourage respectful decision-making or good co-parenting. Legal advice is your lawyers' unique contribution to your divorce. Lawyer time spent driving to court or waiting at a courthouse for your hearing with the judicial officer is not as helpful to the outcome, but it generally costs the same as legal advice.

The two stages of decision making

In many divorce cases, there are two stages in decision making: *temporary* and *permanent*. Thus, there are two agreements or two court orders, as described below. If a couple is making their own decisions, perhaps with the help of a mediator or their lawyers, the temporary agreement may never be filed with the court, or even written down. The temporary issues are the parenting and financial arrangements that will be in place until the divorce happens. When and how to move apart is another part of this.

If the court papers are filed before the divorce decisions are made, the petition may include a request for a *temporary hearing*. (See chapter 7 on "Court Papers" and chapter 8 on "Going to Court" for information on filing for divorce.) If you and your spouse reach an agreement and file it with the court before the temporary hearing, the court will cancel the hearing.

The *final hearing* usually happens about four to eighteen

months after the case is filed. The length of time depends on the disputed issues, the divorcing couple's ability to resolve at least some issues, and the court's schedule. (See chapter 8 on "Going to Court" for details on temporary and final hearings.)

Method 1—the informal approach

For many reasons it is best for divorcing spouses to make their own decisions. They are in the best position to know the details of their relationship. However, this approach is not always possible. Problems in communication are a common reason for divorce. The hurt and anger that are typical of separation and divorce often make discussion difficult. Generally, only the simplest divorces are resolved entirely without the help of mediators or lawyers. And even if you are able to work out all decisions informally, get legal advice during the process.

Most couples can make *some* decisions on their own. Sometimes they can decide one or more of the major issues, such as the parenting plan, leaving other issues to be resolved through mediation, collaborative practice, or negotiation through lawyers.

Many couples can at least resolve smaller issues, such as dividing the kitchen contents, the music collection, or furniture. Every decision you and your spouse can come to informally works to your advantage. It will not only save mediator and attorney's fees, but you will feel better about taking control of these decisions.

In both informal decision-making and other methods, try to speak up for *what you need to get on with your life*, rather than what your spouse owes you. Try to put the past behind you, and focus on the *future*. If you are trying informal decision-making, try to do it in a business-like fashion. Make an appointment with your spouse to talk about a specific issue or related issues. Be sure to meet at a time and place that will insure your child does not hear the discussion. Many couples prefer to go in separate vehicles to a public place, such as a fast-food restaurant.

Most couples using the informal approach work out the agreement first, and then file for divorce. However, the informal method may also be used after filing for divorce.

Even if your agreement is arrived at informally, it must be written down so that you and your former spouse will know exactly what you have agreed to, the court will approve it, and your decisions can be implemented. The best agreements have more details than you think are needed. The details help avoid disputes in the future. Try not to leave loopholes for future misunderstandings.

See appendix B for an explanation of the court's standard paragraphs and what details should be in each.

Method 2—mediation: making decisions with the help of a neutral professional

Mediation is a way for you and your spouse to resolve divorce disputes with the help of an individual trained in techniques for assisting agreement. Such an impartial facilitator is called a *mediator*. Couples sometimes employ a pair of mediators, called *co-mediators*. Mediation uses "interest-based" negotiation. The goal of mediation is to achieve a "win-win" solution, that is, an agreement that meets the basic needs of both parties. Collaborative practice, described in the next section, also has "win-win" as its goal. Most of the positive features of mediation are also present in collaborative practice. Consider both methods before you decide.

Mediation can work even if you and your spouse argue every time you try to talk about divorce. It can work even if one spouse does not want the divorce, and is feeling angry and hurt. In the midst of these feelings, decisions have to be made. The question is who is going to make them. Mediation provides a structure to make the decisions. The mediator's role is similar to a committee chairperson's. Like the chairperson, the mediator organizes and assists with the decision-making process. Most mediators do most or all of the following:

- Explain the mediation process
- Require full disclosure of financial information
- Find out what the issues are
- Help draw up an agenda
- Insure that each spouse presents his or her needs
- Focus attention on the future
- Encourage brainstorming of possible solutions

(In collaborative practice, the lawyers perform similar functions. See a description later in this chapter.)

When selecting a mediator, you should inquire about training, experience, and the individual's approach to mediation. Most mediators and mediation programs will send out information upon request. Some have web sites. New Hampshire has a voluntary program to certify divorce and parenting mediators. State-certified mediators include many lawyers, psychologists and other mental health professionals, and people with other educational backgrounds. Certification is not required to be a mediator. However, even professionals need specific instruction in mediation techniques. The basic mediation training requires forty hours or more. Mediation is not the same as therapy, marriage counseling, or lawyering. More information on certified mediators is available on the state web site. See resources section at the back of this book for details.

Are there different types of mediators?

There are two basic types of mediators: (1) those who have taken a forty-hour training and make communication, future co-parenting, and autonomy of the divorcing couple their priority, and (2) lawyers acting as neutral evaluators who have settlement and avoiding a contested hearing as their goal. The latter process is also called *neutral evaluation*. Select the right type of professional for your family.

What is the court's role in the use of mediation?

The court supports divorcing spouses working out their own agreements. One way the court encourages settlement is to *require* couples to go to mediation. A mediation order is a court order and must be obeyed. The court refers cases to certified mediators who are under contract with the state. The state controls the fees and requires regular reports from the mediator about the status of mediation.

There is also a court-sponsored dispute resolution program called *neutral evaluation*. It is a free service of the court system. The volunteers ("neutrals") who conduct the neutral evaluation sessions are experienced family-law attorneys trained by the court system. This is like mediation in some ways. However, it is different in that the "neutral" may give an opinion on how the case will turn out if a master or judge makes the decisions. Also, neutral evaluation typically consists of one session of three to five hours; mediation usually involves two or more sessions. Some lawyers also provide neutral evaluation services privately, for their regular hourly fee.

How does mediation work?

During the marriage, you or your spouse may have made the important family decisions. Or *you* made certain decisions, and your spouse made others. For example, one of you made decisions about the children and the other made financial decisions. In mediation, the parties make the decisions on divorce issues *together*. Each spouse explains what he or she wants and why. The mediator uses his or her training to see that both spouses participate in the process. The mediator encourages focusing on the future. The goal is to satisfy the needs of each spouse. (Another method using trained professionals to assist joint decision-making is *collaborative practice*, described later in this chapter.)

Mediation requires full disclosure of financial information, so that both spouses can participate in decisions about support, alimony, and property division. Each spouse must be willing to make this disclosure and then must be willing to speak up about his or her needs.

Couples referred to mediation by the court have, by definition, filed for divorce before reaching an agreement. However, most other mediation clients choose to agree first, then file.

What are the advantages of mediation?

Mediation allows you and your spouse to make the decisions for yourselves and your child or children. A mediated agreement can be customized to your family's needs. Many mediated agreements are substantially longer and more detailed than agreements drafted by lawyers. That is because the divorcing couple has more say in the mediated agreement.

A lawyer may criticize part of a mediated agreement by saying, "you don't need this." What is usually meant is "this is not required for the agreement to be *legally* adequate." However, you may wish to retain this part of the agreement for your own purposes.

Perhaps the most important advantage of the process of mediation is that it is one of the two methods (collaborative practice is the other) that are the best preparation for co-parenting after divorce. It may be easier to have your lawyer negotiate your divorce agreement, but if you have a child, you and your spouse will need to communicate and cooperate in the future.

Appendix C lists books on mediation and includes mediation resources.

Why double my costs by paying both a lawyer and a mediator?

Hiring both a lawyer and a mediator will *not* double your costs, because the lawyer and the mediator assist you with different parts of the divorce. In a traditional (non-mediated) divorce, lawyers give legal advice, draft court papers, negotiate or litigate the terms of the divorce, and go to court with you to obtain the divorce. Mediation replaces the lawyer's need to negotiate or litigate the terms of the divorce.

Negotiation or litigation, and the related process of "discovery," are the most expensive parts of the legal process. By making the divorce decisions in mediation, you will save hundreds, or even thousands of dollars in legal fees. In most cases the total cost for hiring both mediators and lawyers will be less than the cost of hiring attorneys alone. (See chapter 5 for more on "Getting Legal Help.")

You have substantial control over both mediator and legal costs. If you can reach agreements with your spouse, both types of fees will be less. If a traditional lawyer-negotiated divorce would cost you (in round figures) $3,000, and instead, you spend $2,000 on mediation (which you split 50/50 with your spouse) and $1,000 on legal services, your total cost would be $2,000. For $1,000 *less*, you have a better quality agreement and a better basis for your future relationship. Your actual cost will, of course, depend upon the fees charged by your mediator and your lawyer, the complexity of your divorce, the number of disputed issues, and the difficulty of reaching agreement.

What is the difference between what mediators and lawyers do in a divorce?

This chart summarizes the key steps in the divorce process, comparing what lawyers and mediators do:

	Mediators	Lawyers
• Give information about the law and the divorce process	yes	yes
• Give advice on legal options for clients	no	yes
• Prepare papers to file for divorce	no	yes
• Assist in reaching the divorce agreement	yes	yes
• Write up the divorce agreement	yes	yes
• Prepare other paperwork required for divorce	varies	yes

As the chart shows, there are several functions common to both mediators and lawyers: furnishing information, assisting with an agreement, and drafting an agreement. However, there are functions that *only* lawyers can offer to clients; these include giving legal advice, and filing for divorce. The most important job that only a lawyer can do is to give *legal advice*. Your lawyer must apply the laws that are appropriate to your family situation and your needs. Since a divorce agreement concerns legal rights and responsibilities, getting legal advice is certainly a good idea! If you ask five mediators what divorce paperwork they prepare and why, you'll get at least three (maybe five) different answers. Some write up the agreement in a form suitable for filing with the court; others do not. Some mediators prepare the child-support worksheet and financial affidavits. Some prepare only the worksheet. Others prepare neither of these forms.

Do I need a lawyer if we use mediation?

Mediation does *not* replace the need for a lawyer in a divorce. It only removes negotiating the divorce agreement from the list of duties that your lawyer must perform. (See the chart on the previous page comparing the roles of a lawyer and a mediator.)

When mediation is used, it is still important to get legal advice. In some mediated cases, both spouses use lawyers throughout the mediation; in others, neither has a lawyer at any point. Perhaps the most common approaches are for only one spouse to have a lawyer, or for each spouse to have a lawyer who has limited involvement during the mediation process. For example, a mediating couple may choose to consult with lawyers only for a review of their mediated agreement. Some people prefer to have a lawyer handle the court paperwork. (See chapter 5 on "Getting Legal Help," and chapter 7 on "Court Papers" for more information.)

Occasionally, some part of a mediated agreement will be unacceptable to the court and will have to be reworked. Getting legal advice early in the process, then having a lawyer review the agreement can usually prevent this. The lawyer can alert you to possible problem areas, suggest changes to deal with them, or attend the hearing to convince the court to approve the agreement.

Fear of lawyers

Sometimes my mediation clients say, "I'm afraid that if I talk to a lawyer, the case will turn into a bloody battle. Is it worth the risk?" In fact, only you and your spouse can turn your divorce into a contested one. The best approach is to select a lawyer who is supportive of mediation and say *up front* that you intend to use mediation. Many lawyers are also mediators and they will support your choice.

Why do mediators suggest that their clients see lawyers? There are several reasons:

- Legal advice enhances the mediation process.
- Lawyers provide different services than mediators do.
- If one spouse is finding it difficult to participate in the mediation process, a lawyer's advice often helps that spouse speak up.

A mediation client once told me, "When I talked to a lawyer several months ago, she wanted to discuss 'what I could get if I had a contested divorce.' This was disturbing, because I wanted to mediate. How can I prevent this from happening if I talk to a lawyer again?" As I explained to that mediation client, lawyers want a client to know *all* his or her options, in order to make an informed choice. If you don't like the lawyer's advice, you can "just say no." If you choose a mediation-friendly lawyer, he or she will understand when you say you have chosen mediation.

Method 3—collaborative practice

In *collaborative practice*, the spouses each work as a team with specially trained professionals to resolve disputes respectfully, without going to court. Collaborative practice is a method similar to mediation, as both methods use "interest-based negotiation." The difference is, mediation uses a neutral to facilitate, while in collaborative practice, the two lawyers facilitate the negotiation in a series of 4-way meetings. The two lawyers and two clients work together to gather information and explore options. As in mediation, the clients make the decisions. Some collaborative practice models use child specialists, financial specialists, and divorce coaches as part of the process.

The essential element of all collaborative models is a commitment to:

- Negotiate a settlement without using the court to decide issues.
- The withdrawal of the lawyers and other professionals if either client goes to court.
- Open information sharing.
- Shared solutions based on the interests of both clients.

How does collaborative practice differ from a traditional divorce?

Traditionally, one spouse sues the other for divorce. Filing the lawsuit begins a series of legal steps. Ultimately, in over 80 percent of divorces, a settlement is reached. But the route to settlement is often a battlefield, with the spouses as adversaries. Conflict is expected, built in to the process. This is harmful to all the family members, but especially the children.

"Making decisions respectfully" is the slogan of the international organization for collaborative professionals. Collaborative practice is a cooperative, non-adversarial way to divorce. The spouses commit to resolving the divorce issues without going to court. Their specially trained lawyers assist, using the cooperative techniques of collaborative practice. These techniques keep the settlement discussions productive.

Once the decisions are worked out, the agreement is written up. The divorce is filed. A collaborative divorce is always "agree first, then file." (If you have filed before learning about collaborative practice, the case may be "withdrawn.")

How does collaborative practice result in a settlement?

Collaborative problem solving and negotiation takes place in structured meetings of the two lawyers and two clients. These meetings are sometimes called "4-ways."

Collaborative practice integrates negotiation with getting legal advice, as your lawyer participates in the 4-way sessions. Generally, lawyers don't participate in mediation sessions.

Each lawyer-client pair meets or talks privately. This happens either between 4-way sessions or during them. The lawyers discuss the case with each other and plan the 4-way meetings, when both spouses and their lawyers meet to assemble information, explore options and negotiate settlement. These sessions are designed to produce an exchange of information and exploration of the needs of each family member.

A focus on the future

Traditional divorce is often caught up in the history of the marriage and its breakup. Pain and anger motivate the actions of one or both spouses. Court papers and hearings are often full of blame.

By contract, collaborative practice is future-oriented. The

future needs and interests of each spouse and each child are a central part of the discussion. The results are both better quality decisions and a smoother transition to life after divorce.

The team model of collaborative practice

Some collaborative cases have one or more other professionals to assist. A *child specialist* can assist with parenting issues. A *financial specialist* can help with sorting out support, asset division, and other financial issues. There may be a *divorce coach* or coaches to assist with emotional issues. These professionals are jointly hired, and commit to work for the family under the collaborative procedures.

Which is best—collaborative divorce or mediation?

A quick answer is whichever method you and your spouse can agree on. Both use "interest-based negotiation" to work out decisions. In mediation, the neutral facilitates the negotiation; in collaborative practice the lawyers jointly facilitate.

Is collaborative practice faster? Cheaper?

By focusing on problem solving, collaborative practice can be a more efficient way to divorce. Full disclosure of information without the adversarial tactics typical of traditional divorce saves time and money.

Method 4—negotiation through lawyers

In most divorce cases couples reach an agreement through their lawyers. This process is called *negotiation*. It often works this way: one spouse gives his or her lawyer information about any agreement which the couple has worked out, along with a list of how the client wants the other issues resolved. The lawyer draws up a proposed agreement, or stipulation. The lawyer and client work together to revise and perfect the agreement. When they are both satisfied, it is sent over to the "other side." The other spouse and his or her lawyer review the agreement and propose changes.

There may be several rounds of negotiation, with a number of draft agreements. Negotiation may take weeks or even months. The lawyers may talk by phone or in person. In some cases, there is a four-way meeting of both of the lawyers and both of the clients. Negotiation through lawyers may use an "agree first, then file" approach or the case may start with one person filing for divorce (or both filing a joint petition).

It *is* possible for the negotiation process to work with only one lawyer. However, the ethical rules for lawyers state that *a lawyer can only represent one spouse.* Thus, the other spouse will have no legal advice.

The method of negotiating with an unrepresented spouse varies from lawyer to lawyer. Some attorneys are hesitant to talk with a self-represented (*pro se*) spouse. (*Pro se*, pronounced "pro say," means "for oneself" in Latin). Other attorneys will not talk at all with a *pro se* party. I am of the latter school of thought. If the other spouse is *pro se*, I use e-mail or mail for all my communications. In fact, most of my negotiations with other lawyers are in writing. (It is my antisocial streak. Some days, I don't want to talk to anyone.)

Negotiation is successful in the majority of cases. The result of a successful negotiation is an agreement which both you and your spouse are willing to sign. This signed agreement is filed with the court. Unless some part of the agreement is unusual or is contrary to New Hampshire law, the judge will approve it. It will be a court order.

Method 5—contested cases: the court decides

Some couples are unable to agree on several or all of the terms of their divorce. Instead, they use litigation. In these cases the master or judge decides the issues, after a contested hearing. "Contested" means that the spouses cannot agree, and thus the court must make the final decision. If there is a *partial* agreement or stipulation, the court will decide the remaining issues. If there is a partial parenting plan, the court decides the disputed parenting issues. The court also decides when one spouse "defaults" by failing to formally participate in the divorce.

The "court" is usually a *master*, a lawyer experienced in family law and a full-time state employee. The master is appointed by the Judicial Branch to hear domestic relations cases. The master holds hearings and makes decisions in family cases. Sometimes a judge hears the case instead of a master. (See chapter 8 on "Going to Court" for more details.)

Only about 10 percent of divorces involve contested final hearings. A contested hearing is *not* the best choice to resolve family problems; the master or judge cannot possibly know as much about the family and its needs as the family members do. However, after efforts to make decisions, if one party is unwilling to reach a reasonable agreement, the other may decide to have the court make the decisions.

Given the emotional and financial costs, and your lack of control over the outcome, try to avoid a contested hearing. Give at least two of the other methods a try before you give up. And if your first effort to settle fails, try again later in the process. In most divorces, one spouse has been considering divorce for months, or even years. The other spouse needs time before he or she is ready to negotiate a settlement.

Temporary issues, final issues

Divorce decisions are usually made in two stages: temporary and final. The temporary issues include:

- Who will move out of the family home?
- How will your child be cared for and supported?
- How will the family's financial needs be met?

According to the court's required Standard Paragraphs Order for Temporary Hearings, there are eighteen temporary issues (see appendix B). If you have a minor child, you must also have three other required forms; a parenting plan, a child support worksheet, and a uniform support order which adds details on child support, health insurance for the child, and payment of the child's uninsured costs.

Most couples either work out the temporary issues and file an agreement, or decide that their informal temporary arrangement is sufficient. The court usually sends those who have contested temporary issues to mediation. If mediation is inappropriate or unsuccessful, a temporary hearing is scheduled. More temporary hearings than divorces are contested. Often, this is because the temporary hearing is scheduled so early in the case.

Temporary hearings last about thirty to sixty minutes. Usually, only the lawyers speak, but if a person is appearing *pro se* (without a lawyer), he or she may speak. (See chapter 7 on "Court Papers" and chapter 8 on "Going to Court" for details.)

After the temporary agreement or hearing, there is typically a period of at least three to six months during which the parties live under the temporary agreement or order. This time is used to gather information and exchange it with the other side. As a practical matter, this period also allows the spouses to adjust financially and psychologically to living apart. This is especially important if the couple was still living together when the case started. It is difficult to go from living together to working out a permanent agreement without a period of living separately.

Court rules set out several methods of *discovery*, formal methods for requiring the other side to provide information. The most commonly used are *interrogatories*, written questions that must be answered under oath. (See chapter 7 for more on discovery documents.) A *deposition* is another type of discovery. The person being deposed must answer questions orally as they are asked by the other side's lawyer.

The court does not automatically schedule a final hearing. (A contested final hearing is also called a "hearing on merits" or "merits hearing.") Usually, the court waits for one of the lawyers to request it. It is usual to try to come to an agreement before a final hearing is scheduled. The agreement may be reached by the parties without assistance, by mediation, or by negotiation. The desired result is a permanent agreement or stipulation, which becomes the basis of the divorce. This means that there can still be an uncontested divorce, even after a contested temporary hearing. (See chapter 8 on "Going to Court" for details.)

What are the disadvantages of having the court decide?

There are several serious disadvantages to having the court decide the divorce issues for your family. These include *higher costs, substantially more time, unpredictability of results, and negative effects on children.* Legal expenses increase significantly in a contested hearing. To understand how costs can vary depending on how you and your spouse make decisions, consider the following comparisons. An ordinary divorce case could have attorney's fees in the following ranges:

- If settled informally, $500–$1,500
- If settled in mediation, $200–$1,000 (plus mediation fees)
- If settled in collaborative practice, $1,000–$5,000
- If settled by negotiation, $1,000–$5,000
- If decided in a contested hearing, $3,000–$10,000

Depending on the number and the complexity of issues, the lawyer's hourly rate, and the level of anger and bitterness between the spouses, the costs listed above may increase by 100 percent, or more. If parenting is disputed, each side will probably have at least $15,000 in attorney's fees, maybe $20,000 or more. Fees in a contested divorce can get to $30,000 or $50,000 if fighting continues.

A contested case may drag on for many months, and even years. There are additional court papers, procedures, and hearings. Contested divorces are routinely allotted two hours for the final hearing. This is enough time only if the disputed issues are small and few in number. If the case is more complicated, it will be scheduled for a half day, a whole day, or multiple days. Two-hour contested hearings are usually scheduled about two to three months in advance; longer hearings are scheduled as much as five to nine months after they are requested. (See chapter 8 on "Going to Court" for details on hearings.) If the case is settled, no hearing is required for the uncontested divorce.

Reaching an agreement and avoiding a contested temporary or final hearing requires compromise, but at least you and the other side have had a say in the parenting and financial details. If the *court* decides, the result may be what one spouse wants, what the other spouse wants, somewhere in between, or even something quite different which the master considers fairer. In other words, a contested hearing is a *gamble*. You do not know how it will turn out. Neither does your spouse. Costs and delays are the only certainties.

Can I appeal, if I don't like the decision?

The case can be delayed still further (and costs escalated) if either side is so unhappy with the final decision that he or she asks the New Hampshire Supreme Court to review it. The Supreme Court changes only a few divorce cases each year. In most cases, the Family Division's decision is approved after a two to six month delay. (See chapter 15 on "Appeals" for more about the appellate process.)

What are the advantages of reaching an agreement?

The case will be over! If you and your spouse sign an agreement, neither side may appeal. Certainty replaces speculation. You will know what you have, and what you have to do. You can get on with your life.

If you and your spouse have a child, even an adult child, an agreement has further advantages. A contested hearing increases hostility between the parents, which adds to the child's stress. If the case ends with a contested hearing, that unpleasant memory will stay with you and the other parent for years. An agreement, even if it takes months to mediate or negotiate, is easier on your child and is a better foundation to your future relationship as co-parents.

We have been fighting over parenting for years. Is there a way to stay out of court?

Even if you have gone to court repeatedly over issues about the children, it can stop. Two alternate dispute resolution methods are available in these cases: mediation, described earlier in this chapter, and parenting coordination. Parenting coordination is for parents who have a parenting plan and need help in making it work. It includes three functions: education, mediation, and arbitration. The specific functions agreed to become part of a court order that spells out the parenting coordinator's role and payment of fees. The parenting coordinator must have training in mediation and in the unique function of parenting coordination.

"Arbitration" means that if mediation does not resolve the dispute about carrying out the parenting plan, the parenting coordinator makes the decision. Parenting coordinators are appointed by agreement of the parents. The arbitration (decision-making) power of the parenting coordinator is limited to disputes about carrying out the parenting plan and other minor parenting issues. The parenting coordinator may *not* change primary residence, the amount of child support, or other key issues that only a court may decide.

getting
legal
help

5

Chapter 5

Getting Legal Help

GOING THROUGH A DIVORCE WITHOUT getting any legal advice is like driving to Alaska without looking at a road map. You might make it to Anchorage, but you will probably get lost several times, miss out on some of the sights you wanted to see, and if your car breaks down, minor inconveniences could turn into real risks.

Under New Hampshire law, marriage, civil union, and parenthood bring both rights and responsibilities. Divorce affects these legal rights and responsibilities. Thus, it is important to find out about the law and how it applies to your situation. The only way to do this is by getting legal advice. A lawyer's legal advice is your road map.

What is a lawyer?

A lawyer is a person who is authorized by a state Supreme Court to advise and represent others in legal matters in that state. A lawyer must have four years of college and three years of graduate education, pass a rigorous bar examination on specific areas of the law, pass an exam on legal ethics, and satisfy a character investigation. Lawyers regularly attend educational seminars and read cases and articles to keep up with changes in the law. New Hampshire lawyers are required to attend at least twelve hours of continuing professional education seminars annually.

Lawyers are subject to ethical rules and supervision by the New Hampshire Supreme Court. The ethical rules are called the Rules of Professional Conduct. Violation of these rules can result in the Supreme Court suspending or removing the lawyer's license to practice.

Many lawyers have malpractice insurance, which protects the client if the lawyer should make a serious mistake, other than one of judgment. There is also a New Hampshire Client Protection Fund established to make restitution to clients for criminal acts by lawyers.

Other people offering "legal help" do not have to meet any of the requirements for lawyers. They may even charge a fee for documents or services you can get for free. If a person who is not a lawyer prepares a legal document for you and it contains an error or is missing some vital words, you are responsible. You will have no one to complain to or sue, even if the error costs you or your family thousands of dollars.

Why do I need a lawyer?

"Do I really need a lawyer to advise or represent me in my divorce?" My answer is that anyone facing a divorce should at least consult a lawyer. Only a lawyer is qualified to give legal advice. The cost of one or two hours of a lawyer's time is an excellent investment and you will at least learn about your rights and responsibilities. Legal advice is especially important if you have children, substantial assets, or if one person doesn't have enough income to be self-supporting.

The sort of legal help you need depends on your family situation (children, income, assets) and how difficult it is to resolve the required issues. You may need two hours of legal counsel and document review. You may need representation through months of litigation. Most people facing divorce need more than two hours but less than months of litigation. This chapter will help you get the amount and type of lawyering you need.

Many serious post-divorce legal problems can develop when a person does not have a lawyer for the divorce. Such problems can be more costly than if a lawyer had been involved in the first place. Without a lawyer, an individual may unwittingly agree to unfair terms, or to an agreement missing essential provisions. I've had many "after divorce" cases where my job is to fix problems that arose because there was no prior legal advice.

It is not a good idea to advise your spouse not to get his or her own lawyer. Any pressure to not get legal advice can cause trouble later, maybe even invalidate a divorce agreement. This is particularly so if it is the spouse with a higher income or a greater knowledge of finances who discourages the other spouse from consulting or hiring a lawyer.

Some people believe that if they use mediation to decide the disputed issues, there is no need to consult lawyers. However, most divorce issues are legal issues. If one or both spouses don't know how New Hampshire law applies to their family situation, the resulting mediated agreement may be unfair or may fail to include a legally necessary provision. At a minimum, a person using mediation should have a lawyer review the mediated agreements before they are signed.

The cost for legal services needed in a mediated divorce is much less than if the lawyer negotiated or litigated the same issues for the spouse. This is because the most time-consuming, and thus the most expensive, part of a divorce is the process of making decisions. (See chapter 4 for more information on mediation and the different functions of lawyers and mediators.)

Can we use the same lawyer?

Can one lawyer handle the divorce for both people? Not in New Hampshire; it is considered unethical to do so. One lawyer cannot represent the different and conflicting interests of both spouses in a divorce. It is possible for one lawyer to represent the spouse filing the divorce, and for the other spouse to choose not to be represented by a lawyer. But the unrepresented person should at least consult a lawyer about his or her rights in the divorce.

How do I find a lawyer?

Hundreds of New Hampshire lawyers regularly handle divorces. The Internet is an excellent source of information about legal services for divorce. Using search engines, you can find names of divorce lawyers and information on lawyers whose names you get from friends or other sources.

Some lawyers will give a free half-hour appointment to potential new clients. Others charge either a small set fee or their regular hourly rate for initial consultation. Once you have several names, call up each lawyer's office and ask about the availability of appointments and the cost of a consultation.

During this initial office consultation, you can get the answers to your basic questions and consider whether this lawyer is the right one for you. Don't expect to get advice over the phone from a lawyer who doesn't know you.

If you are low-income, you may qualify for a free or reduced-fee lawyer to handle your legal problem. Call the Legal Advice and Referral Center at **1-800-639-5290** or **224-3333**, to see if you qualify.

What are the types of legal services available to help with my divorce?

There are 3 forms of legal services:

- Unbundled legal services
- Unbundled legal services with a limited court appearance
- Full representation

Unbundled legal services is a way of buying just the legal services you need, like picking out dishes in a cafeteria line. It could be a one-time service, such as reviewing an agreement you have worked out in mediation. It could be representing you through months of negotiation, using collaborative practice or other method.

You should have a written agreement with your lawyer saying what services she will provide—writing letters, preparing court papers, coaching you in mediation, negotiation—whatever is appropriate for you. Basic unbundled legal service does not include the lawyer going to court for you. This keeps the costs down, because of the time required for repeated court hearings. The savings is both in the initial deposit to hire the lawyer and the total lawyer fees.

Unbundled legal services with limited appearance means what is described above, plus the lawyer attending a specific court hearing. Why would you choose unbundled with a limited appearance? Perhaps your spouse has filed court papers raising a difficult or complicated issue. Or you may need the court's protection due to domestic violence or a threat to an asset.

Full representation is the traditional way of hiring a lawyer for a divorce. It includes all the legal services that are needed through the time the divorce is granted. This may mean several court hearings or conferences.

If you start out with unbundled services but your case turns out to require litigation, your lawyer may agree to change to litigation services, or she may refer you to a litigation lawyer.

How can I find the right lawyer?

Selecting the right lawyer for your family law case is important to the outcome and your satisfaction. The right lawyer is one who:

- has the appropriate education and experience for your case,
- is available when you need advice or representation,
- offers the services you need,
- offers financial terms you can meet,
- makes you feel comfortable about discussing difficult issues, and
- proposes an approach to your case that you agree with.

You can get some of this information by checking the Internet or by calling and talking with the lawyer's staff. If this preliminary information is positive, set up an initial appointment with the lawyer to get the remaining necessary information.

I believe it is best to interview at least two or three lawyers before deciding whom to hire. This is especially important if you have a difficult case, or one involving substantial money. You want to choose your lawyer carefully. The extra advice you get from talking to more than one lawyer will also help you know what to expect from your divorce.

What questions should I ask a lawyer I might hire?

There are so many important questions to ask before you retain a lawyer that it is worthwhile to make a list of them and ask the same questions of each lawyer. Compare their answers, as well as how comfortable you feel as you consult with each lawyer. Here are some general questions to ask:

1. Do you have any specific training in family law?
2. What percentage of your cases are family law?
3. Do you represent or advise more men or more women in divorce cases?
4. What is your view of mediation? Would mediation be appropriate in my case?
5. Do you offer unbundled legal services when appropriate?
6. Are you trained in collaborative practice?
7. Would collaborative practice or other unbundled legal services be appropriate in my case?
8. Will you send me copies of letters and court documents you write and receive?
9. Do you use a written agreement with your clients that explains fees and the client's responsibilities and yours?
10. What do you charge per hour you spend on a case?
11. Would a paralegal, a law clerk, or other lawyers in your firm be working on my case? If yes, what hourly rate would apply?
12. How much money will I have to pay up front?
13. What can I do on my own to help reduce my legal fees?

You should also ask questions about your immediate concerns and issues specific to your case. Write out the questions you want to ask and give each lawyer a copy at the beginning of the consultation.

Collaborative practice and mediation are decision-making methods that promote settlement. Only a lawyer trained in collaborative practice can provide that service. See chapter 4 for more details on decision-making methods. If it is possible that your case will not be settled, ask "How many contested final hearings have you had in the last year? What issues were involved?" Litigators often concentrate on a particular sort of case, such as dividing a small business or allocating parenting rights and responsibilities. You need a lawyer who regularly handles your issues.

However, if you expect (or at least hope) to settle your divorce without litigation, you need a lawyer who supports your goal. If you intend to use mediation to make decisions, ask each lawyer's opinion of mediation. Ask about the type of mediation that emphasizes autonomy and co-parenting (see page 45). Has the lawyer worked with clients who used mediation? Mediation is a new way of resolving divorce disputes. Some lawyers have had no experience or a single negative experience with mediation. As a result, they oppose mediation. If you are going to use mediation, find a "mediation-friendly" lawyer.

Are there some "legal" problems I can handle without a lawyer?

If you represent yourself in a court case, you are said to be *pro se* (pronounced "pro-say"), or self-represented. If you are the victim of domestic violence, you can take action without waiting to get a lawyer. Go to your local District Court or Family Division. The petition for a domestic violence restraining order is user-friendly and there is no fee.

If you have been hurt or threatened, it is easy to get an order for the other person to leave you alone. (See chapter 9 on "Domestic Violence" for more information.)

You may decide to handle other types of cases without being represented by a lawyer. If you want to increase or lower your child support payment, both your local court and the Judicial Branch web site have forms to use. See the "Resources" section in appendix C. Name changes are straightforward. See your local county Probate Court.

Can I represent myself in my divorce?

Under New Hampshire law, you are entitled to represent yourself. If you choose to do so, the court will expect you to follow all court rules. Mistakes can be costly.

Contact your local Family Division court for forms to file for divorce, and for educational programs designed for those considering representing themselves. Case managers and court clerks are helpful, but do not expect them to give any legal advice. The addresses and phone numbers of New Hampshire's Family Division are on the Judicial Branch's web site. Many court forms and information about the court process are also available on the Internet. See the "Resources" section in appendix C.

If you decide to represent yourself and you are unhappy with the result, you will not be allowed to come back with a lawyer and try again! It is your choice whether to represent yourself. Before you do so, at least consult with a lawyer about your rights and responsibilities.

working
with your
lawyer

6

Chapter 6

Working with Your Lawyer

THIS MAY BE THE FIRST time that you have had a lawyer; or maybe you've had a lawyer prepare a will or handle a real estate closing. For most people, a divorce is more complicated and time-consuming than either a will or a house purchase. Thus, the need for legal services is greater.

How can I keep my legal costs down?

Reaching an agreement to resolve your divorce is the most important step in keeping down legal bills. A divorce that is worked out by the spouses will cost substantially less than one decided by a contested hearing. Settlements require compromises. Consider collaborative practice or mediation. (See chapter 4 on "How to Make Divorce Decisions.")

Lawsuits involving family problems are stressful and unpleasant. Divorce is an especially hard time. It is normal to feel depressed, out-of-control, and "crazy." You could benefit from talking with someone with mental health training about your feelings and your family problems (but see the warning below). Your health insurance may help pay for such visits. Community agencies have sliding fee scales or flexible payment plans. Some clients join divorce support groups. Your lawyer is trained to help you with *legal* problems, not emotional problems.

Focusing on settlement and taking emotional issues to an

expert are the most important ways to keep costs down. But making efficient use of your lawyer will save both your time and your money.

What are the first steps in working with my lawyer?

You need to understand the financial terms you have agreed upon with your lawyer. These should be spelled out in a *retainer letter, fee agreement, client agreement,* or similar document.

The basic principle is this: you are paying for your lawyer's time whenever your lawyer works on your case. This includes office visits, phone calls with you or the other side, writing court documents and letters, receiving and reading e-mail and mail, planning strategy, and going to court. Find out how often your lawyer sends out bills, and when each bill must be paid. Be sure that you know what charges your lawyer makes for other staff members, and for expenses such as mileage, phone, faxes, and express mail. With this information you can make the best use of your budget for legal expenses.

At the beginning of your case, your lawyer will ask you to supply certain information. Many lawyers ask each new client to fill out standard forms. As the case goes ahead, your lawyer may ask for more information, financial records, and your comments on various documents. Some of the information requested may be very personal; such as the date you last had sexual intercourse with your spouse. Most lawyers ask for a "history of the marriage." This can be a painful assignment, but it is an efficient way for your lawyer to get the background for your divorce. The financial information may take considerable time to gather and assemble. You must lay out your monthly budget. You may also need to get details on your retirement plan or supply your tax returns for five years.

If you provide requested information completely and promptly, you will not need to pay your lawyer to send you reminders, or to use other methods to get it. If you have problems with the "homework assignments" from your lawyer, call your lawyer's paralegal, law clerk, or secretary. These staff members can often help you provide the information your lawyer needs to represent you.

What papers should I keep?

Getting a divorce is a bureaucratic transaction. You will receive e-mails, letters, and court papers from your lawyer. It is important that you keep all the letters, court papers, and other documents in an organized way, arranging them by date and type of document. Some of my clients use a series of file folders with labels. Others use a three-ring binder with dividers for the different types of documents. Or store everything electronically on your laptop. You may have to assemble various financial records for your lawyer. Always keep a copy for your own file of anything you give your lawyer. Keeping all the important papers will help you work with your lawyer.

How can I make the most efficient use of my lawyer?

The best way to give your lawyer most types of information is to write it down, then mail, fax, or drop it off. Writing is especially good for the history of the relationship, e-mail, summaries of conversations with your spouse or former spouse, and updates of your expenses or income. Of course, if the information is urgent or you need to discuss the information with your lawyer immediately, you may need to call.

Simply dropping in to talk to your lawyer is not an efficient way to work with him or her. Your lawyer may not be in the office when you visit, or may be tied up with an appointment or an urgent project. If you need to talk to your lawyer, call first or e-mail, explain the reason and ask for a phone or office appointment. Tell the lawyer's assistant why you are calling, or give him or her the information you want your lawyer to have. This gives your lawyer a chance to prepare to talk with you. Remember that you have only one case, while your lawyer has dozens and cannot be expected to recall the status of each one.

Before calling or coming in for an appointment with your lawyer, make lists of things you want to discuss or questions you wish to ask. If you are organized, it will take less time to cover the important topics. Give your lawyer a copy of your list of questions. (Better still, e-mail, fax or mail it in before the appointment.) You should also have your file of all the documents on the case with you when you phone your lawyer or go to your lawyer's office. This way you can easily refer to any document in the case.

How can my lawyer's staff help?

Many attorneys have both support staff and paraprofessional staff who help with their cases. By using the staff for matters that do not require your lawyer's time, you will get faster, more economical service. "Support staff" includes those with titles like administrative assistant, secretary, receptionist, and file clerk. Support staff can provide you with basic information about hearing dates, the status of documents drafted by your lawyer, and whether the other side has replied to your proposal. For example, if you want to know when your court papers will be ready to be signed, the secretary will usually know. Use the support staff to leave messages, make appointments, and check on billing questions.

"Paraprofessional" refers to legal assistants, law clerks, and paralegals. Each of these job titles is used for persons with some legal training who are not lawyers. They can do many things lawyers can do, but are not permitted to give legal advice or represent a client in court. Paraprofessionals must work under the supervision of a lawyer. If such a person, or anyone who is not a lawyer, is advertising legal services, it may be a violation of the law.

Paraprofessionals work with clients on various projects, including preparing the financial information needed for court. They can answer many questions about what is scheduled for an upcoming hearing, the status of your case, and the purpose of court papers. Because they don't usually go to court, paraprofessionals are much easier to reach than your lawyer. In some offices, the secretary acts as both secretary and paralegal.

Telling the truth

It is essential that you tell your lawyer the truth. Telling the truth to your lawyer doesn't mean simply not lying. It also means volunteering *all conceivably relevant information.* Your lawyer cannot adequately represent you unless he or she has all the facts.

Because this principle is so important, Anglo-American law developed the concept of "attorney-client privilege." This means that if you tell your lawyer something in confidence, he or she cannot be forced to reveal what you said. Even the fact that you consulted or hired a lawyer is confidential. The only exception to confidentiality is if the lawyer believes that the client intends to commit a crime.

What happens if you don't tell your lawyer the truth? It depends on the importance of the lie or missing fact and when it comes out. Even a white lie or a minor omission is like failing to tell your doctor one of your symptoms. You are expecting the professional to do her job with one hand tied behind her back. The white lie is likely to prolong the treatment (or case) and increase your expenses. It will erode the trust between you and your lawyer, and make it hard for you to work together. In my own practice, I "fire" clients who lie, unless it is a very small issue and they report it promptly. If inaccurate information is given to the other side or to the court, it will be difficult for anyone to believe you or your lawyer in the future.

In the worst scenario, your lawyer may quit. A lawyer cannot knowingly allow perjury (lying under oath). If the client lies during the trial, and the lawyer knows it, the lawyer will tell the judge that he or she has to quit because there is a conflict between the lawyer's duty to the client and his or her duty to the court.

What is the "whole" truth that you must tell your lawyer? In a divorce, just about everything is relevant: the affair you had five years ago, cheating on income taxes, assets put in someone else's name, your spouse's belief that you abused your child two years ago (whether true or not). One test is to ask yourself: "what is the worst thing the other side could say about me, whether it is true or not?" Another test is: "what fact or incident would I least like to have brought out in court?" Your lawyer would like to know the answers to both of these questions—before hearing them from the other side—along with any explanation of your side of the story.

The safest approach is to tell your lawyer everything, or at least discuss with him or her what types of information are relevant for the case. Remember, what you tell your lawyer is protected by the attorney-client privilege.

Problems in working with your lawyer

If you have questions about how your lawyer is handling your case, first consider whether your lawyer might have a clearer and more objective view of your case than you do. If you don't like what your lawyer is telling you, it can be hard to decide whether to rely on your lawyer's judgment.

As with any human relationship, a lawyer-client one may run into problems. There may be difficulty in communicating, or a disagreement about how to handle a certain issue. You may think that your lawyer should be taking action, while your lawyer is actually budgeting his or her time, and your money. It is best to raise these issues promptly with your lawyer. Try to work them out.

The best approach is to let your lawyer know that you have questions, or doubts, or need a heart-to-heart talk. If you simply need some facts, or a status report, see if your lawyer's staff can answer your questions. You could send in your questions or topics for discussion and either ask for a written reply or an appointment. Even if you are considering changing lawyers, be frank about how you feel. Give your lawyer a chance to fix the problem.

Are you considering changing lawyers?

Occasionally, it seems like the lawyer-client relationship is just not working. Perhaps you and your lawyer disagree or don't communicate well and you can't resolve this by talking. You may decide that you would be better off with a lawyer who handles cases differently, or one who has more experience in a certain area.

Consider getting a "second opinion" from another lawyer before you make any change. In a second opinion, the lawyer reviews the court papers in your case (and any other pertinent documents) and discusses what he or she sees as your options. Remember that changing lawyers adds to costs and often delays the case. Some lawyers will not take a case that was previously handled by another lawyer. You don't want to end up without a lawyer during a critical stage in your case. The court may refuse to delay a hearing to give your new lawyer time to prepare.

To sum up, let your lawyer know of your doubts and dissatisfaction. Try to fix the problem. Get a second opinion. If you then decide to change lawyers, there are some steps to take:

- Notify your current lawyer in writing that you are changing lawyers.
- Authorize your current lawyer to give your new one any requested documents and information.
- If appropriate, say something positive about your current lawyer's work.
- Pay your current lawyer any outstanding fees or request a refund, if your lawyer is holding a deposit.
- Give your new lawyer a copy of your letter to your current lawyer.
- Give your new lawyer copies of all the court papers and other documents you have.

I have been fired by clients and I have fired clients. In most cases, the breakdown in the lawyer-client relationship was obvious to both of us, and we were both better off.

To summarize, the best ways to work well with your lawyer and keep your legal costs down are to:

- Take your feelings and emotional issues to a trained mental health professional (except as noted below).

- Understand how your lawyer charges for time and costs.

- Provide information promptly and accurately to your lawyer.

- Keep your legal file and financial records organized.

- Use your lawyer and his or her staff efficiently.

- Make a list of your questions for each appointment with your lawyer.

- Tell the truth.

- Be open about doubts or problems that may arise.

- Be reasonable in working out disputed issues with your spouse.

A warning about counseling records!

Be warned that in most parenting cases and some cases involving fault grounds, your spouse will be able to obtain your counseling records. Do not be surprised if this happens! If parenting or fault are, or may become, part of your divorce, get legal advice before you get or continue counseling.

court
papers

7

Chapter 7

Court Papers

GETTING DIVORCED IN NEW HAMPSHIRE requires some specific legal documents. If you have a minor child or children, there are additional documents required. Cases with many issues and those that result in contested hearings usually result in dozens of documents.

If you use the "agree first, then file" procedure described in chapter 4, all the court papers will be prepared at one time, when the agreement is written up. One reason most divorcing Granite Staters hire a lawyer is to prepare and file the necessary papers. If you decide to represent yourself, you should have a copy of the court rules for divorce cases and the list of standard paragraphs in agreements and parenting plans. The rules outline the court procedures, including the court papers needed at various stages.

What court papers are needed if we agree on the divorce issues?

If all the divorce issues in the case are settled, one of the lawyers will prepare a divorce agreement. If you use mediation, the mediator will prepare a mediated agreement. If the mediated agreement contains all the necessary information, it may take the place of a divorce agreement; or one of the lawyers can put the terms of the mediated agreement in the proper form. If you have a minor child or children, you must work out and file a parenting plan. Any agreement or parenting plan filed in court must be in the standard paragraphs order. (See appendix B.)

Each side must file a financial affidavit. If there is a minor child or children, the court requires a child support worksheet, uniform support order (USO), and standing order. Parents must also attend the child impact seminar and submit proof of attendance.

QDROs (retirement plan orders) and QMCSOs (children's medical insurance orders) are filed only if needed under the terms of the agreement. Frequently, they are filed after the divorce is granted.

What document is used to request a New Hampshire divorce?

The legal document that requests a divorce is a *petition for divorce*. (If the goal is a legal separation, or other domestic relations orders, there are different petitions.) The petition may be filed by either spouse or jointly. The court also requires a personal data sheet with each petition.

The petition may be a fill-in-the-blanks form available from the court or from the state court web site (see "Resources" section in appendix C). The petition can also be drafted by the filing spouse's lawyer. A petition drafted by a lawyer can contain more information on the family, the requests in the petition, and the reason for the requests. An individually drafted petition is more flexible and can be longer than the two-page court form.

The spouse who files the petition is called the *petitioner*. The other spouse is called the *respondent*. If you and your spouse file a joint petition, the person whose name is first on the petition is the petitioner and the other spouse is the respondent. The petitioner (or her lawyer) must also file a vital statistics form, which may be completed online and printed out for filing.

In the "agree first, then file" procedure (see chapter 4), the petition (usually a joint petition), personal data sheet, and vital statistics form are all filed with the divorce agreement, parenting plan, and financial affidavits.

When may a joint petition be used?

You and your spouse may file a *joint petition* if you agree on all the facts stated in it. This must include agreement on the grounds for the divorce and what the issues are. However, it is not necessary that you have an agreement on how to resolve the issues before you file the joint petition.

You may file jointly even when you know that you disagree about one or more issues. For example, one of you might want to sell the house immediately and the other might wish to keep the house.

The rest of this chapter applies to cases that at least start out contested. If you are able to "agree first, then file" you may stop reading here.

Are there special rules if I want alimony?

If you want alimony, you must request it in a court document. This is usually done in the petition for divorce. If you are the respondent, you may request it in an answer or *cross-petition*. Either spouse may also request alimony in a motion filed after the petition.

Are there special rules if the petition says that adultery caused the marriage to break down?

If a petition or cross-petition is based on adultery, the name and address of the person with whom the spouse is accused of adultery must be given, if known. If the information is not known, this fact must be stated. That individual (called *co-respondent*) must receive a copy of the court papers if he or she lives in New Hampshire.

What does the court do when the petition is filed?

When the petition is filed, the court assigns a *docket number* to identify the case. All future court papers must include this docket number.

After the court receives the petition, it issues an *order of notice*. The order of notice gives instructions to the lawyer who filed the papers and to the recipient of the papers. However, there is no order of notice if the parties file a joint petition, or if the respondent agrees to get the petition without being served by the sheriff.

At the beginning of the case, the court issues an *automatic restraining order*. This prohibits either party hiding or disposing of assets. Violation of this order may have serious consequences.

I received a petition filed by my spouse. What are my options?

A good first step is to consult a lawyer about your rights and responsibilities. (See chapter 5 on "Getting Legal Help.") It is important to remember that even if your spouse files a petition for divorce, it is likely that you will work out an agreement to settle the case. Most cases are settled.

The order of notice that the court attaches to the petition tells the recipient that he or she may file an appearance. An *appearance* is a form to tell the court that you want to have a say in the court's decisions. If you hire a lawyer, your lawyer will file the appearance.

If the respondent does not file an appearance (or have a lawyer do so), he or she has "defaulted." Failing to file an appearance may have serious legal consequences. The court can make orders on all the divorce issues, without any input from the person who has defaulted.

You may decide to file an *answer* to the petition, if you disagree with any part of it. You may decide to file a *cross-petition*, with your own requests. If you want alimony, you must request it with a cross-petition or motion.

How is a temporary hearing scheduled?

At the *first appearance*, most cases are referred to mediation to settle both temporary and final issues. In cases with no minor children, this happens at the *scheduling conference*. If the judicial officer is convinced that mediation is inappropriate at this stage, a temporary hearing may be scheduled. (See chapter 8 on "Going to Court" for more details on temporary hearings.)

What documents are needed if you work out the temporary issues?

If you and your spouse can reach an agreement, it is filed with the court and no temporary hearing will be needed. (See chapter 4 on "How to Make Divorce Decisions.") An agreement to resolve the temporary issues may be called a *temporary stipulation* or *temporary agreement*. If you have a minor child, you must file a parenting plan. Any agreement or parenting plan must be written in numbered paragraphs according to the standard paragraph order required by the court. (See appendix B.)

If the temporary agreement includes child support, you and your spouse must also file a uniform support order and the related standing order. The *uniform support order* is a fill-in-the-blanks form required by the court. It contains a summary of the agreement on child support, alimony, the child's health insurance, and uninsured costs. The *standing order* is an attachment to the uniform support order. It contains standard language that applies to all support orders, unless an exception is spelled out in the uniform support order.

If child support or alimony, or other financial issues are involved, each party must file a *financial affidavit*. This is a fill-in-the-blanks form containing details on income, assets, debts, and monthly expenses. It is available from the court or from the state court web site. The court prefers that the financial affidavit be on green paper, as the official form is green.

If no agreement is possible, what documents are required for a contested temporary hearing?

For a contested temporary hearing, each side must file a proposed temporary order, as well as a financial affidavit and proposed parenting plan and uniform support order, if you have a minor child. The proposed temporary order, parenting plan, and uniform support order set out what that person is requesting from the court. Court rules require that the proposed orders and plans be in numbered and lettered paragraphs corresponding to the standard paragraphs. After the hearing, the court will issue a temporary order or decree and a parenting plan, if there is a minor child.

What are "discovery" documents?

Interrogatories are formal written questions prepared by one lawyer for the other side to answer under oath. Under court rules, each side may ask up to fifty questions. They are used in most cases which are, or may become, contested.

Failing to answer interrogatories on time may have serious consequences. Court rules allow thirty days to answer interrogatories, but the deadline is sometimes extended. If the deadline is missed, the other side may file a *motion for conditional default*. This motion is granted automatically by the clerk's office. Once the conditional default is approved, the other side has ten days to supply the answers. Failure to reply within ten days can result in a *final default*. This has the same effect as failing to file an appearance. The court may decide all of the issues without input from the defaulted spouse.

Requests for production are similar to interrogatories, except the goal is to get copies of documents rather than answers to questions. Another type of discovery document is a *request for admissions*. This is a list of facts that the other side is to admit or deny.

Responding to discovery documents is time-consuming. However, fighting the request is rarely successful, and failing to respond can result in losing the case. In most cases, the best approach is to assemble the requested information for your lawyer to send to the other side.

What are "motions" and "objections?"

A *motion* is a request to the court filed during the case. The document contains a description of the reason for the request and what the court is being asked to order. The request may be one that could have been made in a petition or cross-petition at the beginning of the case. The court has a fill-in-the-blanks motion form.

The other side usually replies by filing an *objection* giving his or her view of the issue. The court decides some motions based on the court papers. Other motions are the subject of hearings. (See chapter 8 on "Going to Court.")

What court papers are required for a pretrial conference?

If there is a pretrial conference, a *pretrial statement* must be filed. This document follows an outline set out in the court rules and listed on the hearing notice. Pretrials also require each side to file a proposed final order and financial affidavits. (See chapter 8 for more details on pretrial statements, final orders, and financial affidavits.)

If we have a contested final hearing, what court papers are needed?

For a contested final hearing, each side must file a *proposed final order* or *proposed decree*. The proposed final order and proposed parenting plan set out what terms that spouse wants the court to grant. They must follow the numbering of the standard order of paragraphs. (See appendix B.)

As described above, if there are issues of property division, alimony, or child support, financial affidavits and uniform support orders are required. Proposed QDROs and QMCSOs may be filed with the proposed final order or after the divorce.

Usually, lawyers also submit *requests for findings of fact and rulings of law*. This document sets out the facts and legal principles that the lawyer believes support his or her proposed order. The purpose of requests for findings and rulings is to guide the court concerning the order that side is requesting.

What happens if we agree only on some issues?

If you agree on only some of the issues, you and your spouse may file a *partial permanent agreement* containing the agreed-on issues. Each side must file a proposed final decree, covering the disputed issues. The same procedure applies to the parenting plan. File a partial parenting plan showing what is agreed to and a proposed parenting plan on the other issues. All these documents must follow the standard paragraph numbering. The appropriate financial court papers are required. There will be a contested hearing on the disputed issues. The court's decree will approve the partial agreement and decide the contested issues.

What are the documents used after the contested hearing?

It is very rare for a judge to give a decision orally. Instead the court's decision is set out in a *decree* or *order*. This is mailed out to each side by the clerk's office. The final decree of divorce will become effective thirty days after the date it is mailed, unless other court papers are filed.

If either side wants to challenge the decree, that side may file a *motion for reconsideration* or a *motion for clarification*. This must be filed within ten days of the date the decree was mailed out. Either of these motions will delay the effective date of the divorce.

A reconsideration asks the court to change the decree for one or more stated reasons. A clarification asks the court to clear up some part of the decree or to deal with an apparent conflict between two sections of the decree. The court rarely changes the order based on a motion for reconsideration. Clarifications are more often successful.

Either side may appeal the trial court decision to the New Hampshire Supreme Court. The court paper to start an appeal is a *notice of appeal*. (See chapter 15 for details on appeals.)

going
to
court

8

Chapter 8

Going to Court

IF YOU CHOOSE THE "agree first, then file" approach described in chapter 4, you may never have to go to court, or may go only to file your court papers. (This can be done by mail, but some people choose to hand-deliver the court papers.)

This chapter discusses many technical terms. If you are not sure what a term means, please refer to the "Definitions" section in the back of the book.

What is a hearing?

Events at court that deal with divorce are usually referred to as hearings or conferences. The word "trial" is not generally used. *Hearings* concern the divorce issues or disputes about procedures. *Conferences* concern procedures in the case, including scheduling. The result of a hearing or conference is a decision about the case or some part of it. The parties involved in a divorce (or other family case) and their lawyers, or sometimes just the lawyers, appear before a master or a judge.

Most divorce hearings are conducted by a *master* (a judicial officer authorized to conduct hearings). Masters are specialists in deciding family cases and are employed full time by the state. They are lawyers who have a family law background and who sought the job knowing the types of cases involved.

A hearing or conference may last from two or three minutes to several days, depending on the issues. Most hearings are held in a public courtroom, with other lawyers, clients, and members of the public present. If you wish to have friends or family members attend for moral support, you may do so (but no children). Occasionally, the parties may want the courtroom closed, so that the hearing is private, but such requests are rarely granted.

Each court has a *clerk of court*. The clerk and her deputies are responsible for administrative work, including the scheduling of hearings and conferences. This schedule is called the *court's calendar*.

Going to court usually means waiting!

Most matters having to do with court involve the art of waiting. Here are some of the varieties:

- Waiting to get a hearing date
- Waiting to see the master or judge when you get to court
- Waiting for the decision

Patience is a good virtue to cultivate. Court calendars are crowded and the wait for a hearing can be a month to a year, depending on the type of hearing requested. It is easier for the court to find a five- to thirty-minute opening for a short hearing, than to find a three- to seven-hour opening. The wait also depends upon the workload and the staffing in the particular county or courthouse.

Waiting inside the courthouse is commonplace. You may use some of this time to meet with your lawyer. (You are paying for his or her time.) Bring someone to talk to or something to do: a book, a project from work, or crossword puzzles. For the afternoon there may be a separate list of cases. Occasionally, a hearing doesn't happen on the scheduled day and is rescheduled.

Waiting for the decision is usually the hardest part of waiting. Do not expect a decision the day you go to court. This rarely happens, except on television. Usually the master or judge writes the decision, it is processed, and then the clerk mails out the written order. If the hearing was short and simple, the decision may be out in one or two weeks. For longer and more complicated hearings expect to wait one to three months.

There are different kinds of court events

Court events include: a first appearance, temporary hearings at the beginning of a case, motion hearings to resolve problems that arise during the case, conferences that deal with structuring and scheduling the case, and final hearings. The various types of hearings and conferences are explained in this chapter.

What is the "first appearance"?

This is the first court event. A group of couples with minor children are scheduled for a first appearance at the same time. The judge or master explains the divorce procedure, choices on how to make divorce decisions, and the harm to children of a contested divorce. If you have questions about the procedures to get a divorce, you can get answers. Court staff gives those who have worked out their divorce the necessary paperwork. Most couples are referred to mediation. Cases that need a temporary hearing have one scheduled. See chapter 4 for details on mediation. Cases without minor children begin instead with a scheduling conference.

Temporary hearings

The *temporary hearing* is usually the first hearing in the case. It determines the orders that will be in effect until the final orders are granted. If the case drags on or circumstances change before the divorce is final, there may be another hearing and a new temporary order.

Temporary hearings are scheduled about six to eight weeks after a case is filed. The temporary hearing decides issues such as: temporary parental rights and responsibilities, the parenting schedule, support, use of the home, and payment of bills. Since divorces can take six months or a year, the divorcing parties often need some preliminary decisions about these issues so that they can conduct their lives with some measure of certainty and order until the final hearing.

Usually the information presented at a temporary hearing is on *offers of proof*. This means that each lawyer summarizes what his or her clients and witnesses would say, if the court allowed testimony. Only the lawyers speak. If a person is appearing *pro se* (without a lawyer), he or she gives the "offer of proof." Each side in the case has a limited time specified on the hearing notice. The clients and witnesses do not speak, but must be in the courtroom (including witnesses to *pro se* cases). Each lawyer gives a summary of the case, and of the testimony and evidence that would be presented if there were time for witnesses.

To help the master or judge decide the temporary issues, each side prepares certain court papers, such as a proposed decree, proposed parenting plan, financial affidavit, and child support worksheet. (See chapter 7 on "Court Papers" for details.) The decision on a temporary hearing usually arrives in two to four weeks. The court typically has a "structuring conference" at the same time as the temporary hearing.

Scheduling conference

The first court event in cases without minor children is a *scheduling conference*. The scheduling conference will be scheduled early in the case. The purpose of a scheduling conference is to plan the steps between the conference and the final divorce. In cases without minor children, referrals to mediation are made at the scheduling conference. The court will want to know:

- What are the disputed issues?
- How much time is needed to gather and exchange information?
- Would counseling be helpful?
- Is a guardian *ad litem* needed?
- Would mediation, neutral evaluation, or another alternative dispute procedure be helpful?
- When should another court event occur? What type of event?

Bring your calendar to court!

Motion hearings

Another kind of hearing that may happen before the final hearing is called a *motion hearing*. It deals with matters such as:

- A violation of the temporary order
- A request to change the temporary order
- Procedural issues necessary to get the case ready for the final hearing

A *motion* is a request to the court for a certain action or "relief" (order). A motion for contempt is one example.

Some types of motions are decided based on the motion and objection without a hearing, including motions for reconsideration and motions for conditional default. Most motions are decided after a hearing or conference at which only the lawyers speak. Sometimes, the court hears testimony from the divorcing couple or others. This is called an *"evidentiary hearing."* Motions for contempt often require testimony from the person (not the lawyer) filing it. Motion hearings may take ten minutes or several hours, depending on the issues.

Status and case management conferences

If the court thinks it would be helpful, or if either side requests it, the court may schedule a *status conference* or *case management conference*. The purpose of these is to find out what is happening in the case and, if possible, to expedite it. These conferences usually are set when very little has happened for several months.

Pretrial conferences

A *pretrial conference* is a special type of hearing to prepare the case for a contested final hearing. Usually, the pretrials are held in the courtroom; sometimes, they are held in the master's office with only the lawyers present. The clients must be present in the courthouse, unless they have been excused by the court (because they live out of state or for some other valid reason). Each party must file certain documents at the pretrial, including:

- Pretrial statement (this may be agreed-on and filed jointly)
- Proposed order
- Financial affidavit

- Child support worksheet (if there is a minor child)
- uniform support order and standing orders (if there is a minor child)

See chapter 7 for more information on "Court Papers."

The "*pretrial statement*" that must be filed at the pretrial includes:

- A list of disputed issues
- A list of property in dispute, and whether there will be appraisals (valuations)
- Any special circumstances justifying a variation in child support guidelines
- Any factors justifying sole decision-making responsibility
- Any factors justifying an unequal property division
- Any factors to be considered in an alimony award
- Names of expert witnesses
- Names of other witnesses
- A list of any pending motions
- Any problems about exchanging information
- The length of the trial
- Whether alternate dispute resolution or another method of settlement has been or will be used
- Factors that may affect the scheduling (such as an out-of-state witness)
- Whether either party wants a record made of the final hearing

The parties must also give each other copies of the documents. This gives each more information on the other side's case. During the pretrial, the master and lawyers (or *pro se* party) review the case, the issues, the number of witnesses, and any information which must still be exchanged. If an issue is not listed at the pretrial conference, it may not be brought up at the final hearing.

The court will make a pretrial order, which includes how long the trial will be (two hours, half day, one day, etc.) and who the witnesses will be. By agreement, or if the court believes it will be helpful, the order may set up a neutral evaluation. This is a process similar to mediation. (See chapter 4 for details on neutral evaluation.)

At the pretrial, the date or dates for the contested final hearing is scheduled. This is usually on the next available date that can accommodate the length of time required. If the hearing is to be for two hours, the judicial officer looks for the first date suitable for a two-hour hearing. If the time period is a half day or longer, the date is usually several months in the future. A date is selected when parties and counsel are available. (Bring your calendar to the pretrial.)

Settlement conferences

If the court thinks it would be helpful to the case, or if either side requests it, the court may schedule a *settlement conference*. The purpose is to resolve disputed issues and thus avoid a contested hearing.

Sometimes cases are settled at the pretrial conference or shortly after. At this point, everyone should have enough information to settle. The reality of a court date, or how far in the future it is, can encourage settlement.

Final hearings

A *final hearing* decides whether or not there will be a divorce, and results in an order (decree) resolving all the issues. There are two categories of final hearings, uncontested and contested. Uncontested hearings usually take five minutes or less. There are two types of uncontested hearings:

- Default: one spouse has not participated in the case
- Stipulated: settled by agreement

Most cases are stipulated and this usually means no final hearing at all. Both spouses sign an agreement (*stipulation*), and parenting plan if there is a minor child. These documents resolve all of the issues. Both spouses must submit financial affidavits, unless neither support nor property division is an issue. If you do not have a lawyer, it is wise to talk to the clerk's office before filing your papers, since the procedure for getting an uncontested divorce varies from court to court.

In stipulated cases, upon request, and if the court thinks it is appropriate, the divorce may be granted without a hearing. One way to request this is to include it in a written agreement. Some courts require a motion that states why a hearing should not be required. Your court clerk's office can explain the local procedure.

If there is a hearing in a stipulated case, only the spouse seeking the divorce and his or her lawyer need to go to court. The divorce is effective within one week.

What if my spouse defaults?

In a defaulted case, the other spouse does not "appear" (participate in the case), either represented by an attorney or *pro se* (for himself or herself). Failure to respond to discovery requests may also result in a default. The master or judge only hears one side, the spouse who filed for divorce. The lawyer will prepare a proposed order for the master or judge, listing what that spouse wants. The divorce is effective in approximately thirty days.

Contested final hearings

Contested final hearings (also called *merits hearings*) occur in about 10 percent of divorces. The hearing may take from one hour to several days. Each spouse gives testimony under oath about the marriage and how the disputed issues should be resolved. Each lawyer asks questions of both his or her own client and the other spouse. Either side may present additional witnesses and submit evidence to support a request. Many court papers must be filed. (See chapter 7.)

In a contested hearing, legal expenses increase considerably. After hearing both sides, the master or judge decides the disputed issues. It usually takes somewhere between fourteen and sixty days to get the order. The divorce and other terms are effective thirty days after the court issues them, unless one or both sides file papers to question or appeal the order. (See chapter 15 on "Appeals.")

Preparing to go to court

Most people are nervous and uncomfortable when they have to go to court for their divorce case. This is a normal reaction. The best way to handle this is with careful preparation.

A visit to the courthouse prior to the date of your hearing will help. Courts are open from 8 a.m. to 4 p.m. Ask your lawyer, or the court clerk's office, what day or time would be best for your visit. Sit down as an observer and watch other divorce hearings. This will give you a more accurate understanding of how divorce cases are handled in New Hampshire. An advance visit also gives you the chance to check on details that might get in the way later: how to get there, where to park, and where the courtroom is. If it is not possible to attend other divorce hearings, at least drive to the court on a day prior to your hearing, and check the route and parking.

Your lawyer will want to talk or meet with you to prepare for the hearing. Depending on the type of hearing and the topics to be covered, this may mean only a brief phone call or a short meeting at the courthouse on the day of the hearing. If it is a contested final or other major hearing, the preparation may mean several office appointments or a day-long meeting.

Your day in court—what to bring

You should bring to court your file of court papers on the case. One week before the hearing, take time to review all these papers. Put them in chronological order, in either file folders or a notebook.

Bring with you any records or documentation concerning the topics that the hearing is about. For instance, if the hearing is about a parenting dispute, bring your log or diary about the parenting schedule. If the dispute concerns support payments, bring your records of support checks received and the dates. If you are the parent paying support, bring your canceled checks or other documentation. If the hearing is to establish or change the amount of support, bring several recent pay stubs, and your prior year's tax return.

Bring all your checkbook records, bank statements, and

canceled checks for the last twelve months, so you can prove your expenses, if asked. Your lawyer may ask you to bring other items. Take time to organize your court papers, receipts, and other records so you can easily find a specific paper if you need it during the hearing.

Do *not* bring to the courthouse anything that the metal detector or the bailiff (court security officer) would see as a real or potential weapon: guns, knives, penknives, knitting needles, mace, nail files, scissors, and so on. Most courthouses prohibit food. All purses, briefcases, and other containers will be searched. Leave unnecessary items at home or locked in your car.

Do I have to testify?

Clients do not always have to testify at hearings. At temporary hearings or conferences, only the lawyers speak. (If a person does not have a lawyer, he or she is allowed to speak.) Frequently, hearings on motions consist of brief statements by each lawyer. Despite the fact that you may not speak, I recommend going to court for each hearing, unless you cannot afford the travel time or income loss. It is the best way to know what is happening in your case. In any event, you must go to the hearing unless your lawyer says it is not necessary.

What do I need to know about being a witness?

It is essential that you tell the truth in court papers you sign, including the financial affidavit and any interrogatories, and when you testify under oath. Telling the truth in court means giving truthful answers to the questions you are asked. You are not required to volunteer additional information that the lawyer didn't request in the question. However, if the lawyer insists on a yes or no answer and such a short answer might mislead those who are listening, you should insist on being allowed to explain your answer.

Lying under oath is perjury and a crime. I know of divorce cases where individuals (not my clients) lied about their incomes or assets, and were later charged with and found guilty of perjury. This means a criminal conviction, and jail. And if this is not enough to convince you, think about the loss of credibility. If the judge finds out you lied on one point, or hid information, all of your testimony is going to be suspect.

The side that requested the hearing or filed for divorce goes first. If the clients are to give testimony, one client is questioned by his or her lawyer and then by the other person's lawyer. Sometimes, a lawyer will also call the other lawyer's client as a witness. The choice of witnesses and in what order they testify is part of the strategy of the case.

"Calling a witness" means the lawyer says to the judge, "I call (name of witness)." If your name is called, walk to the witness stand, a chair near the Judge. When you get to the witness stand, the lawyer who has called you will swear you in. "Do you swear that the testimony you are about to give will be the truth, the whole truth, and nothing but the truth, so help you God?" (The "so help you God" part is optional, as is the "swearing" part, if you find it objectionable.) You answer, "I do." For this swearing in you should stand up and raise your right hand. As soon as the oath is finished, you may sit down.

The series of questions asked by the lawyer who called the witness is called the *direct examination*. In direct examination, the lawyer generally must ask questions that do not suggest the answer he or she is seeking. For example, "Did you and your spouse have any understanding about the role each of you would have in the marriage?"

Listen carefully to each question and then answer that question, not the question you would like it to be! Speak clearly, with enough volume so that the judge and the lawyers can hear what you are saying. Tell the truth.

What is cross-examination?

Questions asked by the other lawyer (other than the one who called you as a witness) are the *cross-examination*. In cross-examination, the lawyer may ask "leading questions" that suggest the answer. For example, "You agreed that your spouse should stay home and take care of the child, didn't you?"

When the opposing lawyer asks you questions, be polite. Answer each question, without furnishing extra information. The only exception to this is if the opposing lawyer insists on a yes or no answer, and you cannot give such an answer without an explanation. If this happens, you should give the explanation.

Remember, every question asked by the opposing lawyer is designed to get you to say something that will be helpful to the opposing party. Witnesses often want to be agreeable and helpful in responding to the opposition's questions. This is usually a mistake. If you don't agree with every part of the question, don't answer "yes." If you do not know or don't remember the answer, say so firmly. If you know or remember part of the answer, say so and tell what you know.

While you are being questioned, the other lawyer may object by standing up and saying "objection." If this happens, you should stop talking, even if you are in the middle of a sentence. An *objection* means that there is some legal dispute about the question being asked or the answer being given. The judge will decide if the question or answer objected to was proper. All of this can be confusing to the witness. If it is not clear to you whether you are to answer the question, simply turn to the judge and say, "Am I supposed to answer the question?" If you've forgotten what the question is, ask the lawyer to repeat it.

Chambers

Something that can be confusing or puzzling to clients is when both lawyers go into the master's (or judge's) office and do not reappear for a considerable time. The master's office is called his or her "chambers," and this kind of event is called a *chambers' conference*. It is routine to have a chambers' conference before the hearing. The master and lawyers may preview what will be presented at the hearing, and in what order. They discuss any disputed legal principles. Occasionally, there is a chambers' conference during the hearing. This gives the judge a chance to comment on how the hearing is proceeding and to ask how much time will be needed to complete it.

An uncontested hearing

An uncontested divorce may be granted without a hearing. If there is a hearing, the person who filed the divorce and his or her lawyer appear briefly before the master or judge. This can either be in chambers or in the courtroom. After swearing the client in, the lawyer asks a few basic questions to give the court the information needed for the divorce. If there is no attorney, the master or judge will ask the questions. The questions usually include:

- Were you married to (spouse's name) on (date of marriage)?
- Have irreconcilable differences caused the irremediable breakdown of the marriage?

- Briefly, what are the irreconcilable differences?
- Is there any way to repair the marriage?
- Did you sign this agreement voluntarily?
- Do you want this agreement to be the basis of your divorce?

What should I wear to court?

Clients often ask about what to wear to court. You should dress neatly and conservatively. I recommend that men wear a suit or a jacket and tie (or at least a dress shirt and tie) with slacks. If you never wear ties, a neat solid color shirt would be fine. For women, a suit, tailored dress, or skirt and blouse would be appropriate (nothing dressy or tight-fitted). Neat, tailored slacks are fine. No jeans or tee shirts for men or women.

Courtrooms are frequently either overheated or excessively air-conditioned. Layers of clothing are better than a heavy sweater or a short-sleeved blouse or shirt. Be well groomed with neat hair and conservative makeup. No chewing gum!

∞

domestic
violence

9

Chapter 9

Domestic Violence

VIOLENCE IN THE HOME IS a crime, but has traditionally been viewed as a private matter. This cultural bias, along with threats of retaliation by the offender, has made wives, girlfriends, and other abuse victims hesitant to seek help. When men are victims, they are often too embarrassed to seek help. Fortunately, in New Hampshire, we have two types of resources for domestic violence victims: a progressive statute that makes it easy to get help from the police and the courts, and local support groups that provide information and counseling. If you are a victim of domestic violence, you may get a court to issue a *restraining order*.

What is domestic violence?

Domestic violence victims may include spouses, former spouses, sexual partners, those involved in a romantic relationship, parents, and other relatives of the violent person. ("Elder abuse" of senior citizens by family members is on the increase.) Domestic violence includes rape, physical injury, threats to injure, destroying property and unauthorized entry. It also includes *attempting* to do any of these things.

If you have a problem with your own anger, or have been violent toward your spouse, please seek help from a therapist with appropriate training. You can change your life (and your child's) by putting an end to violence.

A related problem is stalking, defined and discussed at the end of this chapter. The same support groups and counselors who work with domestic violence also address stalking.

What is a restraining order?

New Hampshire's domestic violence statute is a civil, rather than criminal, statute. A restraining order says that the other person must leave you alone and not enter your house or apartment. Under the domestic violence statute, the order may include terms that:

- Direct the police to take weapons from the abuser
- Concern custody and child support
- Concern use of home, car, and other assets

Having a court order makes it much easier to get help from the police if you have future problems with the same person. Also, if the abuser violates the order, it is a criminal offense.

Any District or Family Division court may issue a temporary domestic violence order. There are no filing fees. You don't need a lawyer to get a restraining order and most people do not have one when they file. For more information on your options, call the twenty-four hour domestic violence hotline at 1-800-852-3388.

How can I get a restraining order?

It is best to go to the District Court or Family Division, but you should call first. There may be a specific time when domestic violence cases are taken care of. If you live in a small town without a court, call your town police to find which District Court or Family Division courthouse handles cases from your town.

In most courts, you can see a judge and get a temporary

order the same day. On evenings, weekends, and other times when courts are closed, an emergency order is available with the help of your police department. When the courts are closed, the order is issued by telephone. If you get your order by telephone, the next day the court is open, you must go to court, or the order will end.

How does the other person find out about the restraining order?

After you receive a domestic violence order, the court faxes it to the police to be served on your attacker. There is no fee for this service. It is helpful to provide specific information on where your abuser is (or will be). The orders take effect only when the abuser is served.

What happens at the final hearing?

The court will schedule a final hearing for a few weeks after the date of the emergency order. The date is written on the domestic violence order. It is essential to go to this hearing. If you don't go, the restraining order is canceled. The purpose of the final hearing is to give both you and the other person a chance to tell your side of what happened. (If your abuser doesn't show up, the judge will grant your request to extend the restraining order.)

You should bring to the hearing any of the following that you have:

- Witnesses
- Medical records of injuries from the abuse
- Police reports
- Photographs of injuries
- Letters, e-mail, or other documents concerning the threats or violence

- Evidence of financial losses you have had because of the violence
- Estimates of damages related to the abuse
- Documents or information about your child, or your need for child support

Be prepared to tell the judge about the incident and any prior violence or threats. If you and the abuser have minor children, explain what you want for custody, visitation, and support orders. It helps to prepare an outline or summary of what you want to say in court, so you won't leave out anything important. If the judge concludes that you have proven that you have been abused, he or she may issue restraining orders good for up to one year. After one year, if you still need a restraining order, you can ask the court to extend it.

Where can I get more information?

Help is available in New Hampshire from various local domestic violence support groups. You can find the nearest group by calling 1-800-852-3388, twenty-four hours a day. These groups have trained staff who provide information and support for abuse victims. These people can provide psychological support, explain how to file a domestic violence petition, and sometimes even go to court with you. (Also see the "Resources" section in appendix C.)

The New Hampshire Bar Association sponsors the Dove program to supply volunteer lawyers to domestic violence victims at final hearings. Call the Legal Advice and Referral Center (LARC) at 1-800-639-5290, to see if you qualify.

Should I consult a lawyer?

While you don't need a lawyer to get a domestic violence restraining order, you should consult a lawyer if:

- you have been severely injured, or
- you expect the injury to last, or
- either you or your spouse is seeking a divorce.

Can I file criminal charges?

In addition to getting the restraining order, you may file criminal charges against your abuser. Consider any negative side effects this may have before taking this step. You may want to talk to a lawyer or a domestic violence support group before acting.

If the attack was within the past six hours, the police may arrest the attacker and file the charges. Otherwise, you may file the original criminal complaint yourself. Blank complaint forms are available from the police and from the District Court. Describe the incident, and write the number of the statute (RSA) that was violated. A good source for information on bringing criminal charges is the domestic violence pamphlet put out by New Hampshire Legal Assistance. To get one, call 1-800-562-3174.

Once you have filed the criminal complaint, the police department (or the county prosecutor) brings the charges against your attacker. You may not withdraw the complaint and get the case dismissed.

Can I get my spouse to move out without getting a domestic violence order? What happens if domestic violence petitions are misused?

Unless you have been hurt, or fear for your physical safety, a domestic violence order is not appropriate, especially if the person you accuse is the other parent of your child. This can have a serious impact on your relationship. Making up a story about your spouse, or exaggerating an incident is wrong and may be a crime. Additionally, lying under oath is the crime of perjury.

If you want your spouse to move out because you are getting a divorce, there are other ways to accomplish this:

- Talk it out with your spouse.
- Use counseling.
- Use mediation or collaborative practice (see chapter 4).
- Negotiate through your lawyers (see chapter 4).
- Ask the divorce court for a "move out" order.

As part of the temporary order in a divorce, the court may order that one of the spouses move out. It is not necessary to have been a domestic violence victim to get a "move out" order. The usual reason for a move-out order is that the tension between divorcing parents is harmful to children.

What is stalking?

In plain language, *stalking* is following or shadowing another person in an intimidating fashion. New Hampshire law provides three legal definitions of stalking:

- Following another from place to place on more than one occasion:
    - for no legitimate purpose, with the intent to place the person in fear for his or her personal safety, or
    - under circumstances that would cause a reasonable person to fear for his or her personal safety
- Appearing on more than one occasion, for no legitimate purpose, close to the residence, place

of employment, or other place where another person is:

— with the intent to place the person in fear for his or her personal safety

— under circumstances that would cause a reasonable person to fear for his or her personal safety

- After receiving notice of a protective or restraining order prohibiting contact with a specific individual, violating such order by:

— following another person from place to place

— appearing in proximity to any place described in the order

If I'm being stalked, can I get a protective order?

The procedure for a protective order is the same as for a domestic violence order. For more information on protection from stalking, contact a domestic violence support group or your local District Court or Family Division. Stalking is also a crime. A stalker is subject to arrest by any law enforcement officer. The New Hampshire Coalition Against Domestic and Sexual Violence offers a brochure on stalking. (See "Resources" in appendix C.)

parenting—
the law

10

Chapter 10

Parenting—The Law

IN NEW HAMPSHIRE, THE LAW recognizes that children do best when both parents have a stable and meaningful involvement in their lives. The policy of the state is to:

- Support frequent and continuing contact between each child and both parents.

- Encourage parents to share in the rights and responsibilities of raising their children after the parents have separated or divorced.

- Encourage parents to develop their own parenting plan with the assistance of legal and mediation professionals, unless there is evidence of domestic violence, child abuse, or neglect.

- Grant parents and courts the widest discretion in developing a parenting plan.

- Consider both the best interests of the child and the safety of the parties in developing a parenting plan.

Exceptions (to the policy described above) are made only if it is clearly shown that in a particular case this state policy is detrimental to a child.

When parents divorce, they must prepare a parenting plan explaining how they will share the care of their child or children. Because of the public policy to encourage shared parenting, the concept of "custody" has been abolished.

Instead, the parenting plan explains how decisions will be made, includes a parenting schedule spelling out in detail the time the children will be with each parent, and describes other parenting functions.

What is a parenting plan?

A *parenting plan* is a written plan describing how the parents will share responsibility for their child or children. This includes decision-making procedures, the weekly and holiday schedule, information sharing and access, transportation and exchange of child, relocation, and procedures for adjustment of the plan. See appendix B for a detailed list of parenting plan topics.

For web sites and books that can help in developing a parenting plan for your child or children, see appendix C.

How is the parenting plan decided?

Most parenting plans are drawn up by the parents. This is the most desirable method. The parents know and love the child or children. If you and your spouse can make the parenting decisions yourself, your children will benefit greatly.

Mediation is one method for parents to work out a parenting plan and make other divorce decisions. You can choose to start the divorce process by going to mediation. Or, if you start by filing in the court, the court can order parents to mediation. In mediation, a trained neutral person assists the parents in making decisions for their children. *Collaborative practice* is another good decision-making method for parents. The divorcing couple work as a team with trained professionals to resolve disputes respectfully. Both of these methods support co-parenting after the divorce.

Review chapter 4 for help in deciding what method would be best for your family.

What is decision-making responsibility?

Decision-making responsibility is the legal right to make important decisions for the child. Most family law attorneys agree that it includes the right to participate in important decisions, to see school and medical records, and to give consents for health care. While New Hampshire law provides no checklist of "important decisions," it is likely that educational, medical, and psychological decisions are among the "important" ones covered by legal decision-making responsibility. If a parent has sole decision-making responsibility, that parent can make significant decisions for the child without consulting the other parent.

Unless there has been domestic violence, the law presumes that there will be shared decision-making responsibility. More than 78 percent of New Hampshire divorce cases with children include shared decision making responsibility. However, the parents may agree that one of them will have sole decision-making responsibility, or the court may order it. The usual reasons for sole decision-making responsibility are a pattern of domestic violence, a history of no contact with the child, or an inability to make joint decisions.

What is a parenting schedule?

The parenting plan includes the *parenting schedule*, which defines the time the child spends with each parent. There is no perfect parenting schedule. However, the best schedules:

- are based primarily on the child's needs, rather than the parents' needs;

- include specifics, but allow for flexibility; and
- are adjusted over time, as the child's needs change.

I recommend including some specifics about the weekly schedule, and important holidays and vacations. Even if you and the other parent are working cooperatively right now, there may be times in the future when this breaks down. Having a "default plan" in place, one that can work even if communication is difficult, is in the child's best interest. Having a schedule allows both parents, and the child, to plan ahead. It is helpful to post the parenting schedule on the refrigerator or mark it on the kitchen calendar.

You and the other parent can agree to make one-time (or long-term) changes to the plan. There are no "parenting plan police" to be sure you are observing the Fourth of July schedule or any other specifics in the plan. The written schedule is a default plan, so you are not constantly negotiating with the other parent. Instead, you need only negotiate exceptions or changes to the plan.

Here is a sample that shows some of the specifics that might be included in a parenting schedule for a school-aged child:

A. We shall alternate having the child on weekends from Friday after school to 7 p.m. on Sunday. However, during the summer, the period shall end at 9 a.m. Monday.

B. Monday holidays shall go to the parent with the weekend adjoining the holiday.

C. Father (or mother) shall have the child on weekdays, except that mother (or father) shall have the child one weeknight from 5 to 7:30 p.m., to be Wednesday, unless we agree otherwise.

D. Mother shall have the child for the February vacation in odd-numbered years and the April vacation in even-numbered years. Father shall have the alternate years. Each of these vacation weeks shall be for seven days, including the parent's usual weekend.

E. Mother shall have the child from 9 a.m. to 7 p.m. on Mother's Day and father shall have the child from 9 a.m. to 7 p.m. on Father's Day.

F. Father shall have the child for Rosh Hashanah in even-numbered years and Yom Kippur in odd-numbered years. Mother shall have the child alternate years.

G. In odd-numbered years, mother shall have the child for Thanksgiving from 6 p.m. Wednesday to 6 p.m. Friday. Father shall have the alternate years.

H. Father shall have the child from noon Christmas Eve to noon Christmas Day in even-numbered years and from noon Christmas Day to noon, December 26 in odd-numbered years. Mother shall have the alternate years.

I. Each parent shall have the child for up to three weeks in the summer, during his or her vacation, provided he or she gives notice by 1 April.

What is primary residential responsibility?

Some parenting plans designate a *primary residential parent*, but this is an optional provision. A dispute over something that is optional is not in your child's best interest. All that is required is the parenting schedule.

What is the legal test for a major change in the parenting schedule?

A major change could mean switching which parent the child lives with most of the time.

Unless the parents agree to a major change, New Hampshire law discourages such a modification of the parenting schedule after the divorce. The rationale for this is that stability is important for children.

Without an agreement, the parent seeking a major change in the parenting schedule must show that the child's present environment is detrimental to the child's health and the advantage to the child of changing the order outweighs the harm likely to be caused by a change in environment. This is a difficult test.

There are, however, three special exceptions to this test. If the parents have substantially equal periods of residential responsibility, the "best interest" test may apply. If a "mature minor" (usually at least twelve to fourteen years old) requests a change in the parenting plan, the court is likely to grant it. The other exception is when one parent has repeatedly, and without good cause, withheld or interfered with the other parent's time with the child. (See chapter 16 on "After Divorce" for details on modifying parenting plans.)

Will the parenting schedule change as your child grows?

As a child grows, his or her needs change. School-aged children need a different sort of schedule than what is appropriate for babies, toddlers, and preschoolers. As the children get older, the schedule for school, extracurricular and community activities, and part-time or summer jobs may conflict with the original schedule. In the teenage years, most children want to spend more time with friends and less time with family.

For these reasons, the schedule will need to be adjusted. Some parents build into their parenting plans a yearly, or twice yearly, review or adjustment. This can be a paragraph with many specifics as to where and how parents will conduct the review; or it can be something basic, for example:

A. In July or August of each year, we will review the child's upcoming school year and adjust the parenting schedule as needed.

B. In February or March of each year, we will review the child's upcoming summer and adjust the parenting schedule as needed.

How much may the parenting schedule be changed after the divorce?

Minor adjustments to the plan are expected. One of the parenting plan standard paragraphs is "procedure for review and adjustment of parenting plan." Most plans say that the parents will try to work out such adjustments, or mediate them, rather than going to court. Minor adjustments could include ending the weekend on Monday morning instead of Sunday night, increasing the summer vacation periods, or adding a weeknight overnight. Major changes, such as switching which parent the child lives with most of the time or going to a 50/50 schedule can be made if the parents agree. If only one parent wants a major change, it is more difficult.

What happens if we don't agree on the parenting plan?

Most parents can work out at least some of the seven major

topics (or of the dozens of minor issues) required in a parenting plan. They then file a *partial parenting plan,* showing what they agree on. Each parent also files a proposal for the issues not agreed on.

If parents are unable to work out their parenting schedule, or some other topic in the parenting plan, it will be left to the master or judge to decide. This happens in 6 percent of divorces. Later in this chapter there is information about litigating parenting issues.

What do New Hampshire parenting schedules look like?

Most divorcing couples work out an agreement. An increasing number of families (25 percent) have a schedule that is 50/50 or close to that. At least 52 percent of agreements and orders in divorce have the child (or children) living primarily with mother. At least 7 percent have the child (or children) living primarily with father. In less than 2 percent of cases, each parent has at least one child living primarily with him or her. (In 14 percent of cases, the court records were not clear on the living arrangements.)

More and more couples are choosing a shared parenting schedule. Changes in our society, our laws, and the roles of men and women are reasons for this. What is most important is a schedule that is right for your child and allows both parents to be active in the child's life.

May the parents move apart after divorce?

Divorcing parents often make a commitment to living within a certain geographical area in order to carry out their parenting plan. The plan may include such geographical limits for them, or it may simply require that notice be given before a move is made. For example, the plan might stipulate that neither parent shall move more than thirty miles from the State House in Concord; or that before a move that would increase travel time more than thirty minutes, the other parent shall receive sixty days' notice.

If, in the future, a parent seeks to move, the court may allow it, but only if certain legal tests are met. At this point, the court will consider any wording in the agreement about geographical restrictions and the reasons for them. (See chapter 16 on "After Divorce" for more information.)

Can stepparents, grandparents or others have residential responsibility or visitation rights?

In unusual situations, the court may award residential responsibility to a stepparent or grandparent. As the parent is the preferred custodian, the other person must have a very good reason. Unless there is an open divorce or parenting case, grandparents seeking the care of a child must file for a guardianship in the Probate Court.

New Hampshire law says that grandparents and step parents may seek visitation. If you and the other parent agree on the issue of visitation with grandparents, you can include it in your divorce agreement. You could include a statement such as: "The grandparents shall have the right to reasonable visitation, phone calls, and other contact with the child. This contact shall continue even if one of the parents dies." In a few divorce or parenting cases, grandparents hire a separate lawyer to represent their interests. Most divorce lawyers handle grandparent cases. (See the "Resources" section in appendix C for more information.)

What is the legal test if the court decides the parenting plan?

The legal test will be the best interest of the child. To determine this, the court will likely consider:

- The relationship of the child with each parent and the ability of each parent to provide the child with nurture, love, affection, and guidance.

- The ability of each parent to assure that the child receives adequate food, clothing, shelter, medical care, and a safe environment.

- The child's developmental needs and the ability of each parent to meet them, both in the present and in the future.

- The quality of the child's adjustment to the child's school and community and the potential effect of any change.

- The ability and disposition of each parent to foster a positive relationship and frequent and continuing physical, written, and telephonic contact with the other parent, except where contact will result in harm to the child or to a parent.

- The support of each parent for the child's contact with the other parent as shown by allowing and promoting such contact.

- The support of each parent for the child's relationship with the other parent.

- The relationship of the child with any other person who may significantly affect the child.

- The ability of the parents to communicate, cooperate with each other, and make joint decisions concerning the children.

- Any evidence of child abuse, or domestic violence (abuse) and the impact of the abuse on the child and on the relationship between the child and the abusing parent.

- If a parent is incarcerated, the reason for and the length of the incarceration, and any unique issues that arise as a result of incarceration.

- Any additional factors the court deems relevant.

Parenting fights in court are expensive, exhausting, and disruptive. Each parent may have attorney's fees of $15,000, $20,000, or more. The case may take up to two or three years from the time the case is filed until the final decision. The pursuit of a parenting battle should be a last resort.

The child's preference is rarely a factor, except for teenagers. (See the discussion of "mature minors" in the next section.) There is no preference based on the gender of the parent or of the child. In applying the best interest test, the court looks at the needs of the child, taking into account the child's age and any individual factors.

The court looks at the pattern of parenting established in the family before the separation or the filing of court papers. If one parent has provided most of the parenting, the court may question a request to make major changes in that pattern. This is an especially important factor in cases involving babies and preschool children. However, divorce often means that an at-home parent takes a job, or a parent moves from a part-time to full-time work. These changes usually result in changes in the parenting pattern. There are other reasons the court would not keep the prior pattern in place. If the parent who has been the primary caregiver has abused or neglected the child, it is likely that the children will live primarily with the other parent. The same is true if the primary caregiver has a health problem such as alcoholism, drug addiction, or mental illness, or has moved out, leaving the child with the other parent.

(Note that the law is different for parenting cases that take place *after* the divorce. See chapter 16 for an explanation.)

Can teenagers decide where they will live?

There is an added legal factor to New Hampshire parenting disputes that concern teenagers. A mature minor's opinion is very influential in deciding the parenting schedule, as long as the choice is not based on "improper influences." There is no set age when all children become "mature" for purposes of stating a preference. It is decided individually. Most children become "mature" in the court's eyes sometime between ages twelve and fourteen. Examples of "improper influences" are a parent promising the child there will be no curfew, or that the child will have a car at age sixteen if he or she lives primarily with that parent.

The mature minor does not actually decide the parenting schedule. The court must still consider whether the child's preference would be in his or her own best interest.

What is a guardian *ad litem*?

If the parents are unable to decide on the parenting schedule or some other part of the parenting plan, the court usually appoints a guardian *ad litem* to represent the interests of the child. "Guardian *ad litem*" (pronounced "add-LITE-em") is often abbreviated to "GAL" (pronounced "G-A-L") or simply "guardian." The guardian does not represent the parents. His or her job is to find out the needs of the *child*, and to consider the child's well-being. The court order appointing the guardian spells out the specific issues that need to be investigated, such as parenting skills, substance abuse, living conditions, or physical abuse.

The guardian gathers information about the child's needs and each parent's ability to care for the child, as well as the specific issues listed in the court appointment order. This information is given to the court. Usually, the guardian prepares a written report with his or her recommendations.

How is the guardian selected and paid?

Often the parents' lawyers select the guardian; otherwise, the court will name someone. The guardian is chosen from a list of certified guardians. To become certified, individuals must be trained and meet requirements set by the Guardian *ad Litem* Certification Board. About half of guardians are lawyers, but there are also psychologists, social workers, and individuals with other backgrounds. See www.nh.gov/gal for more information and lists of certified guardians.

The guardian must be paid. Usually the cost is split between the parents. If the parents' incomes are greatly different, one parent may be ordered to pay the entire fee or a bigger proportion of it. Usually the court will order (or the guardian will require) a deposit of $1,000 or more before work begins. Each parent must pay his or her share promptly. At the final hearing, the remaining part of the guardian's fee is allocated by the judge.

If both parents have incomes below specified amounts, the state will pay the guardian's fee. The state may require either or both parents to make payments to help reimburse the state for the cost. Because the state pays guardians less than standard professional fees, the choice of guardians for a state-paid case is limited. Many of the most experienced guardians accept only a limited number of cases paid by the state.

How does the guardian function?

The guardian meets with both the parents and the children. Young children are sometimes seen at home. The guardian will also contact people suggested by each parent. Guardians usually find that teachers, baby-sitters, and pediatricians are important sources of information.

During the guardian's investigation, each parent's behavior

toward the child and the other parent is under scrutiny. It is essential to put the child's interest first. Don't use this time to try to "get even" with the other parent. Most important:

- Do not ask the child where he or she wishes to live.
- Do not criticize the other parent in front of the child.
- Do not let the child see or hear hostile interactions with the other parent.

Of course, these are rules to follow throughout the divorce. (Also read chapter 2 for more information on "Parenting During and After Divorce.")

Are there unhealthy reasons for fighting about parenting?

Divorce is a very bad time for most people. Due to pain, stress, or anger, a parent may behave differently than he or she would normally. Some parents engage in a fight about the parenting schedule for reasons other than the child's best interest. A parent may threaten a fight out of anger about the divorce, or as a bargaining chip in a dispute over child support. (These parents, however, rarely go through with the threat to file such court papers.) Sometimes a parent is driven by guilt or family pressure to put up a fight over the child.

Perhaps the most unhealthy reaction to the pain of divorce is the abduction of the child to another state or country. This is against the law in all states and most countries. It is the court in the child's home community that must decide about parenting. If your child is abducted, get legal advice promptly. Other information about abduction is in the "Resources" list in appendix C.

Summary

Sharing in the upbringing of your child is a privilege. Working out a *fair* agreement is in the best interest of your children. Hostility between you and your spouse may prevent your children from finding a healthy way to deal with the divorce. If the conflict is over the child, it is especially hard for the child to deal with. If it is difficult or impossible for you to work out a parenting plan, seek help from a mental health professional or a mediator or a collaborative lawyer. If the fighting occurs or continues after your parenting plan is in place, consider a parenting coordinator (see explanation on page 60). Think of the benefit to your child or children if you are able to cooperate in their care and upbringing. (See chapter 2 for suggestions on "Parenting During and After the Divorce.")

child
support

11

Chapter 11

Child Support

NEW HAMPSHIRE LAW REQUIRES THE use of a formula called the *Guidelines* in setting the amount of child support. The goals are to provide adequate support for children, and to ensure that parents with similar incomes pay similar amounts of support. Instructions and forms for the Guidelines are available in every Family Division court and on the Judicial Branch web site.

How much will the child support be?

The amount of support is based on a fixed percentage of both parents' incomes. The percentages are:

- One child: 25 percent of net income
- Two children: 33 percent of net income
- Three children: 40 percent of net income
- Four or more children: 45 percent of net income

The master or judge must review any agreement that you and your spouse make to see that the child support is fair under the law. The court may refuse to approve an agreement that does not meet the Guidelines and may deny the divorce. You and the other parent are not free to decide the amount of child support. You must use the Guidelines, unless you convince the court that one of the limited exceptions applies. The exceptions are discussed later in this chapter. If the court decides child support, the Guidelines are used, unless there is a "special circumstance" as described later in this chapter.

The Guidelines first calculate the total amount of support needed for the child or children, then divide the amount between the two parents. Child support is proportional to each parent's available income. "Available" means what the child support Guidelines worksheet says is available, not what the parent has in his or her bank account or wallet.

What information is needed to calculate child support?

The Guidelines are a complicated formula for deciding support. To do the Guidelines, first assemble the following information:

- Pay stubs of each parent
- If either is self-employed, the business tax return or schedule showing:
    - —The gross and net business income
    - —The amount of self-employment tax
- Cost of health insurance for children (The difference between the cost of family plan and the cost for only the parent.)
- Child care costs

Use the pay stubs to determine each parent's gross income, before taxes or other deductions. Gross income includes all income from any source, whether earned or unearned, including commissions, bonuses, pensions, worker's compensation, and other sources. The income categories listed on the court financial affidavit form can be used as a guide. Overtime earnings (beyond forty hours) are excluded if the overtime is "occasional or seasonal" and the worker is paid hourly in an industry which commonly pays overtime.

What is monthly gross income, if I am paid weekly?

The Guidelines calculation uses monthly gross income. It is essential to get the monthly gross income right, if you or the other parent gets paid other than monthly. Don't confuse alternate-week pay (twenty-six times a year) with twice-a-month pay (twenty-four times a year). Here is how to get the *monthly* gross:

- If the pay is weekly, multiply the weekly gross pay by 4.33.
- If the pay is alternate weeks, multiply the alternate week gross pay by 2.17.
- If the pay is twice a month, multiply the twice-a-month gross pay by two.
- If the pay is monthly, just use the number!
- If the pay is a yearly figure, divide the yearly gross pay by 12.

All the deductions must also be changed to monthly figures. Use the appropriate formula from above.

What deductions can I take?

The Guidelines allow certain deductions for expenses. Each of the amounts for expenses used in the calculation must be converted to a monthly amount, as described above. If either spouse pays state income tax, or court-ordered support for others (a prior spouse or children), or mandatory (state or federal government) retirement, subtract these amounts from his or her gross income. Self-employed parents may subtract 50 percent of their self-employment tax.

If the parent paying support (the obligor) pays for health insurance covering the children, or child care costs for the children, that parent may deduct these costs from gross income. If the children are covered by a family plan, calculate the children's cost by subtracting the costs of the parent from the cost of the family plan. The allowable child care expenses have limits or maximums:

- One child: $417 a month
- Two children: $750 a month
- Three children: $1,000 a month

Note that the maximum child care deduction may be less than the actual cost of child care. Even if your child care costs are actually higher, you may only subtract the maximum amount. If the parent receiving support (the obligee) pays for child care or medical insurance, it is subtracted at a later point in the calculation.

Examples, based on sample families

How do the Guidelines work? The following examples may give you a clearer picture of how child support would come out as key numbers are changed:

Example 1 – In this situation, the father (obligor) earns $30,000 yearly and pays $100 monthly for the children's health insurance; the mother (obligee) earns $20,000 yearly; their two children live with her most of the time, and she pays child care costs of $600 monthly. Result: the father pays $169 weekly. *See the sample calculation on page 151.*

Example 2 – If the facts are the same as example 1, except that the father pays for the $600 a month child care, he'll pay $112 a week in support.

Example 3 – If the same facts apply, except that the father has the children most of the time and pays the health insurance and child care costs, the mother pays support of $120 weekly.

Whether or not the parent receiving child support works has only a small effect on the amount of support. In the examples above, if the parent who has the children most of the time was not working (and thus there is no child care), but the working parent provides health insurance, support would be:

Example 1 – $153 a week

Example 2 – $153 a week (same facts as example 1)

Example 3 – $104 a week

How is child support calculated?

To calculate child support you must use a "Child Support Guidelines Worksheet" form. This form, with a sample calculation, is shown on page 151. A child support calculator is available online at **www.dhhs.state.nh.us/DHHS/ DCSS/Child+Support+Calculator/_Entry+form.htm** or can be done by hand as described below using the calculation table available at each court clerk's office.

In filling out the form, remember that all numbers must be monthly. See discussion on converting weekly and alternate week numbers to monthly numbers earlier in this chapter. First, fill in the children's names and dates of birth. On lines 1 and 2, fill in the number of children and the required percentage (the sample shows 33 percent for two children). Enter each parent's monthly gross income on line 3. If self-employed, use net business income. Remember, the parent who will pay child support is the *obligor* and his or her information goes in the first column.

Subtract from each parent's gross monthly income any of the following that apply: support paid for others, mandatory (government employee) retirement, 50 percent of self-employment tax, and for the obligor (parent who pays), medical insurance for the child and child care costs.

The result of subtractions is each parent's adjusted gross income (line 5).

Add the parents' adjusted gross incomes together to get the combined adjusted gross income. To do the next step, you must consult the current year's Child Support Guideline Calculation Table. (As the Table is over sixty pages long, many lawyers have a special software program to do this.) The Table is available for you to use at all Family Division locations. The Table subtracts from the adjusted gross incomes the standard federal income deductions for a single person with two exemptions, plus Social Security and Medicare for the combined income.

To use the Table, find the page and the row on that page that lists the combined adjusted gross income. Go across the row to the column for the number of children the support is for. The Table will give you combined support to be provided by both parents. (Of course, the parent who has the child most of the time doesn't write a support check; he or she houses, clothes, and feeds the child.) The number you get from the Table is entered on line 6.

How is the "combined support" divided between the other parent and myself?

The next step is to figure the percentage of total support each parent must contribute. This is where you subtract any medical insurance or allowable child care costs that the parent receiving support (obligee) pays. The child care deduction is subject to the same maximum amounts discussed earlier in the chapter. The result of any subtractions is the obligee's total adjusted gross income (line 8). For the obligor (paying) parent, the total adjusted gross income is the same as the adjusted gross income that you got earlier in the calculation (line 5).

THE STATE OF NEW HAMPSHIRE
JUDICIAL BRANCH
http://www.courts.state.nh.us

Court Name: Court

Case Name: In the Matter of Andy Sample and Ann Sample

Case Number:
(if known)

CHILD SUPPORT GUIDELINES WORKSHEET

Child's Name	DOB	Child's Name	DOB
child 1			
child 2			

1. Total Number of Children	2	2. Child Support Guidelines Percent	33 %

PAYMENT CALCULATIONS	OBLIGOR	OBLIGEE	COMBINED
3. Monthly gross income	2,500.00	1,666.66	
4A. Court/Admin ordered support for other children	0.00	0.00	
4B. 50% of actual self-employment taxes paid	0.00	0.00	
4C. Mandatory retirement	0.00	0.00	
4D. Actual state income taxes paid	0.00	0.00	
4E. Allowable child care expenses (obligor)	0.00		
4F. Medical insurance for children (obligor)	100.00		
4G. Total Deductions	100.00	0.00	
5. Adjusted monthly gross income	2,400.00	1,666.66	4,066.66
6. Child support guideline amount			1,063.48
7A. Allowable child care expenses (obligee)		600.00	
7B. Medical insurance for children (obligee)		0.00	
7C. Total allowable adjusted expenses		000.00	
8. Total adjusted monthly gross income	2,400.00	1,066.66	3,466.66
9. Proportional share of income	69%	31%	
10. Parental support obligation	733.80	329.68	
ABILITY TO PAY CALCULATION			
11. Self-support reserve	851.00		
12. Income available for support	1,549.00		
13. Monthly support payable	733.80		

14. CHILD SUPPORT ORDER	Frequency (circle one):
(If weekly,divide line 13 by 4.33; if bi-weekly,divide line 13 by 2.17; if monthly,enter the same amount as line 13) **ROUND THE RESULT TO THE NEAREST WHOLE DOLLAR** $169.00	● Weekly ○ Bi-Weekly ○ Monthly

PREPARED BY: _____   DATE : _____

TITLE : _____

NHJB-2101-FS (12/11/2006)   Page 1 of 3

Calculation of child support for *Example 1* on page 148.

For each parent, divide his or her adjusted gross income by the combined adjusted gross incomes. The results (line 9) are the percentages each parent will pay of the total child support. To get the specific amount for the support-paying parent, multiply his or her percentage by the total support amount (see line 10, obligor column).

Lines 11 through 13 are a calculation to be sure that the obligor has a certain minimum amount for his or her own expenses. If income is low, the support may be $50 or even less a month, rather than the amount determined by the guidelines. For most families, this "ability to pay" calculation has no impact. Thus, the amount entered on line 10 and the amount entered on line 13 are the same (see sample).

The result (line 13) is the monthly support. If the paying parent (obligor) is paid weekly, divide the monthly amount by 4.33 to get the accurate weekly amount. If the obligor is paid every two weeks, divide the monthly amount by 2.17. Round off to the nearest whole dollar (line 14).

By this point, you are probably thoroughly confused! Don't worry; it is harder to explain the Guidelines calculation in words than it is to do the calculation. You may find the examples below helpful. If you have a lawyer, your lawyer or his or her assistant will do the calculation. If you use mediation, your mediator will help you calculate the Guidelines. If you are calculating support on your own, the Guidelines Worksheet comes with step-by-step instructions. (But you will need a calculator.) Or use the support calculator on the state web site.

Is there child support on bonuses and commissions?

If the parent paying support receives commissions, bonuses, or income other than salary or wages, support is due on this income. This is usually done by paying the appropriate percentage (25, 33, 40, or 45 percent) of the net amount of the commission or "other" income, when the money is received. The agreement or order should spell out how support on the other income is to be handled.

Are the Guidelines always used?

If the court thinks it would be fair and in the best interest of the child or children, certain "special circumstances" *may* result in the Guidelines not being used, or being adjusted up or down. Even if "special circumstances" exist, the court may use the Guidelines, without adjustments. The master or judge must explain and justify any decision not to use the Guidelines.

These "special circumstances," listed in New Hampshire's child support law, are:

A. Ongoing extraordinary expenses of the child

B. Significantly high or low income of either parent:

    1. In high-income cases, the court reviews the child's reasonable needs, considering the lifestyle at both parents' homes.

    2. In low-income cases, the court determines how to optimize use of the parents' combined incomes for the child, including considering child-related tax benefits.

C. Economic effects of other natural or adopted children, stepparents, or stepchildren

D. Reasonable expenses of the parent paying support in exercising his or her parental rights and responsibilities, provided that the reasonable expenses of the other parent for the children can still be met

E. Disposition of the family home to benefit the child

F. Opportunity to optimize both parties' after-tax income by considering federal tax consequences, including the right to claim the child as dependent.

G. State tax obligations

H. Parenting schedule, in light of the following factors:

1. Whether the parents have divided up the child's variable expenses, such as clothing, education, day care, and health insurance.

2. Does the parenting schedule decrease the lower-income parent's expenses?

3. Can the lower-income parent meet the costs of the child in a similar style to that of the other parent?

I. Economic consequences of college expenses for a natural or adopted child

J. Resulting order is unreasonably low or very high

The law does not explain how to determine support if one or more of these special circumstances exists. This is decided on a case-by-case basis. The master or judge may use a test such as that given in section D above: whether the expenses of the other parent for the child can still be met if the Guidelines amount is adjusted or not used at all. The court may also choose to use the Guidelines without adjustment.

Generally, the reduction in child support is less than the real cost of any item listed above. For example, if you have college costs of $10,000 for another child, the court might adjust your income by only $7,000. If you live in another state and have to fly to New Hampshire to see your child (or fly the child to your home), the court may reduce your child support by less than the total plane fare.

What if the child lives with each parent half of the time?

Such a schedule does not necessarily mean no child support. If the parents have similar incomes and if the parenting time is evenly divided, support might be zero. If incomes are different, or the number of children with each parent is different, or the parenting periods are unequal, support is likely. It could be the full amount determined by the Guidelines, or a lesser amount. See the prior section for the factors considered when the parenting schedule is given as the "special circumstance" to vary from the Guidelines.

What if one child lives with mother and the other child lives with father?

This requires an adjustment to the guidelines. As in the case where each parent has the child half of the time, support may be zero, or the full Guidelines, or something in between.

What is a uniform support order?

Each child support order must be spelled out on a court form called a *uniform support order (USO)*. The uniform support order includes the amount of support, the frequency of payments (weekly, alternate weeks, twice a month, or monthly), and any arrearage (past due amount). The USO also contains a summary of the health insurance, uninsured health costs, and alimony provisions. The USO states who provides the children's health insurance and who pays for their uninsured health costs. If the paying parent is unemployed or if neither parent has medical insurance, the USO deals with those situations. If there is alimony, it is also listed on the USO. As the USO form is also used for paternity cases, there are sections that don't apply in a divorce.

Whenever there is a USO, there must also be a *standing order (SO)*. The standing order includes basic terms concerning when child support changes or ends. If some part of the SO doesn't apply to your case, note this in the uniform support order.

What is a wage assignment?

The uniform support order may require that the support be automatically deducted from the other parent's pay (wage assignment). A support-receiving parent whose current order does not require a wage assignment may have a wage assignment set up. There are two ways to do this:

- Get a court order, or agreement filed with the court.
- Apply to the New Hampshire Human Services Department.

Once you get the USO that provides for a wage assignment, you or your lawyer must send the paying parent's employer. The New Hampshire Human Services Department can be found in the phone book listed under "New Hampshire, State of." In some communities there is a listing under "Human Services" for "Child Support." It takes two to four months to have the state set up a wage assignment, but it is worth doing if support is late or irregular.

If you are the parent paying support, consider agreeing to a wage assignment. It is a convenient way to pay and saves $20 or more annually in postage, envelope, and check costs. A wage assignment also simplifies balancing your checkbook. Your child support obligations are taken care of automatically and unemotionally, and you can focus on parenting your child.

What if the other parent doesn't pay ordered support and misses a payment?

If your spouse fails to make an ordered payment *during* the divorce, you can file a motion for contempt. Judges expect court orders to be obeyed and will make additional orders, if necessary, for a wage assignment, or even a threat of jail. (If you had only an informal agreement on support, it's time to request a temporary order.)

If this problem comes up *after* the divorce, you can seek help from the New Hampshire Human Services Department or reopen the court case. The Department can do one of the following: obtain a wage assignment, including the missed payments; get the other parent's tax refunds from the federal government; seize bank accounts or other assets; suspend driving, hunting, or other licenses. (See chapter 16 for more information on procedures "After Divorce.")

Can child support be changed?

Support may be increased or decreased by agreement or by reopening the legal case. Agreements are simpler to do, but it is important that the agreement be in writing and filed with the court. An informal agreement does not change the existing court order.

If you and your former spouse agree to change child support, the agreement must be signed by both of you and filed with the court. You must also file a financial affidavit for each parent, a Guidelines worksheet, and a uniform support order (USO). If both parents sign the USO, the USO can be the agreement.

If agreement to change child support is not possible, either parent may file court papers to reopen the case. If it has been three years or more since the last child support orders, the court will recalculate support. If it has been less than three years, the person seeking the recalculation must show a substantial change in circumstances, unless the prior agreement or order required more frequent recalculations. (See chapter 16 for more details.)

alimony

12

Chapter 12

Alimony

FOR MANY DIVORCING COUPLES, ALIMONY is a "hot but-ton" issue. One spouse requests alimony and the other refuses to pay, sometimes simply as a matter of principle.

What is alimony?

Alimony is financial support for a spouse or former spouse. It may be either in the form of direct payments to the recipient or payments to others on behalf of the recipient. Alimony qualifies for special tax treatment. (See chapter 14 on "Taxes and Divorce.")

There are three types of important financial decisions to be made in a divorce:

- Child support (see chapter 11)
- Property division (see chapter 13)
- Alimony

All of these decisions may be made either by agreement between the spouses or by court order. Decisions are by agreement in more than 80 percent of cases. (See chapter 4 on "How to Make Divorce Decisions.") If there are minor children, child support is usually resolved first. As the property division can affect alimony, either it should be decided before alimony, or they should be considered together.

Alimony is present in a minority of New Hampshire divorces. There is often no request for alimony. Sometimes it is requested, but there isn't enough money to make it possible. Or the higher income spouse is unwilling to include alimony in the agreement.

In litigated cases, alimony must be formally requested in the divorce petition or another court paper. If there is no written request, the court will not order alimony. If requested, alimony may be included in the temporary order or the final divorce decree, or both. In some cases, the spouses agree or the court orders temporary alimony, to be in effect while the case is pending. At the time of the final divorce decree, alimony may or may not continue, depending on current incomes and needs, and the property division. Alimony most often follows a long-term marriage (say ten or fifteen years or more) or where there are very different earning abilities. Alimony is most common for a household with a high-income husband and a homemaker wife.

In certain other states, including Massachusetts, alimony awards appear to be more common, longer lasting, and larger in amount. There has been no study of what makes New Hampshire different. One factor may be a common misconception that alimony is not allowed under New Hampshire law. Our culture of independence, or gender bias, are other possible factors.

It is important to look at alimony objectively rather than emotionally. Alimony is simply one way to deal with financial matters in divorce. Because of its favorable federal tax treatment, it may be a useful or necessary ingredient of the financial part of your divorce.

Will I get alimony or will I have to pay it?

Since more than 80 percent of divorces are based on an agreement of the parties, it is likely the answer will depend on you and your spouse. Reviewing the test used by the court to decide about alimony may give you some insight. (Ten percent of cases are defaulted, and the court grants the petitioner's requests.)

Will the court award alimony in my divorce?

If yours is one of the 10 percent of cases that are decided by the court after a contested hearing, the following three-part test will be used:

A. The person seeking alimony lacks sufficient income, property, or both, including property received under the property division statute, to provide for his or her reasonable needs, considering the parties' lifestyle in the marriage; *and*

B. The person from whom alimony is sought can meet his or her reasonable needs while paying alimony, considering the parties' lifestyle in the marriage; *and*

C. The person seeking alimony either cannot meet his or her reasonable needs through appropriate employment or has responsibilities for a child of the parties whose condition or circumstances make it appropriate that the parent not seek employment outside the home.

This test for alimony is abbreviated as "need and ability to pay." If one spouse needs alimony and has requested it and the other can afford to pay it, the court may order it. Alimony may be paid in a lump sum, periodic payments (weekly, monthly, or some other frequency) or both. Most alimony is paid in periodic payments.

Even if there is no alimony at the time of the divorce, remember that alimony can be requested up to five years after the divorce.

How is the amount of alimony decided?

If your case is settled, then you and your spouse will decide the amount with the help of your lawyers and CPA. This usually involves looking at projected budgets and income for each. If the court is making the decision, New Hampshire law requires that the following factors *shall* be considered:

- The length of the marriage
- The age, health, social or economic status, occupation, amount and sources of income, the property awarded under the property division statute, vocational skills, employability, assets, liabilities, and needs of each of the parties
- The opportunity of each spouse to earn money and gain assets in the future
- The fault of either party (adultery, extreme cruelty, etc.)
- The federal tax consequences of the order

The court *may* also consider, in setting the amount of alimony:

- The contribution of each spouse in the gaining, preserving, or increasing the value of assets
- The non-economic contribution of each spouse to the family

A final alimony order may be for a specific period, or have no ending date. Alimony for a set period of time allows the spouse to obtain education, training, or work experience so that he or she can be fully self-supporting. In some states this is called rehabilitative alimony, but that term is not used in New Hampshire law.

Alimony may decrease over time, based on the assumption that the recipient will be gradually increasing income.

If the spouse is disabled, or, because of age or health, is unlikely to ever become self-supporting in a style comparable to the marriage, the court may award alimony without any ending date. Either party may later reopen the case to have alimony ended, extended, increased, or decreased.

Because of federal tax law, the alimony provision must say that alimony ends if the recipient dies. The agreement or order may list other factors that either end alimony, or trigger a review of the need for, or amount of, alimony. Some alimony provisions specify reductions on set dates in the future. (For examples, see the section on "specifics in alimony orders" later in this chapter.)

While the "Guidelines" formula determines child support in New Hampshire, there are no mathematical formulae or guidelines for deciding the amount of alimony. In an agreed-on divorce, the amount could be any number. In litigated cases, the Judge or master has wide discretion in determining the amount. Alimony is based on the lifestyle or standard of living during the marriage. (If someone receives an inheritance or wins the lottery after being divorced, the former spouse should not expect to share in this wealth.) The court sometimes uses a method that attempts to "equalize" the standard of living. However, many court orders do not follow the equalization principle. The former spouses may end up with substantially different standards of living after the divorce.

The advantages of alimony

Some people choose to have alimony as part of the divorce agreement because of the federal tax advantages. The paying spouse may deduct alimony payments, but the recipient must treat them as taxable income. If the spouses are in greatly differing tax brackets, this may make alimony a good financial arrangement. The alimony payment may include money to cover the recipient's tax on the alimony. It is also possible for the agreement or orders to provide that the alimony is not deductible and non-taxable.

By contrast, other types of payment that one spouse makes to another because of divorce (child support or property settlement) are neither deductible nor taxable. Sometimes, with the help of tax experts, it is possible to pay alimony rather than a property settlement, and thus get a tax advantage. (See chapter 14 on "Taxes and Divorce" for more specifics.) Note that this is a technical and complex matter. Get advice from a lawyer or a CPA, or both.

Alimony and property division

Sometimes a choice must be made between seeking more of the assets in the property division, and seeking alimony. While assets are usually divided 50/50, the split may also be 60/40 or 70/30 or any other ratio. (See chapter 13 on "Property Division" for details.) If one spouse will be paying the property settlement over time, it is important to consider whether the obligation can be met. A bankruptcy may eliminate property settlement payments, but alimony is not ended by a bankruptcy.

Receiving more of the assets immediately may provide more security in the future than alimony will. Alimony may be ended by court order at some time in the future. In some cases, alimony payments may be late or not made at all. A person receiving the family home or stocks and bonds or cash is more able to provide adequately for his or her own future.

For the higher-income person, there is a risk to trading more assets for "no alimony." After the spouse receives the extra assets, he or she may come back and seek alimony. Some spouses agree that neither of them will ever request alimony, technically called a *waiver*. Under New Hampshire law, an alimony waiver is not enforceable. A person may request alimony up to five years after the divorce. Some judges and masters will not approve a waiver paragraph in a divorce agreement.

For the lower-income person, an unequal property division may not be as good as spousal support. This can be because of the amount of support needed, the amount of assets, or the fact that the nature of the assets limits their use as "support."

The choice of alimony and property division, or a mix of the two, that is appropriate in each case depends on the specific facts. It is important to get legal and tax advice on your options. (Review chapters 3 and 14 on financial planning and taxes.)

Specifics in alimony orders

The divorce agreement or order will state the amount of alimony, the frequency of payments (weekly, alternate weeks, twice monthly, monthly), and when it begins. If the alimony is to decrease over time, the schedule of changes is set out. The agreement or order may state when, or under what circumstances, the alimony will be reviewed or will end. Whatever the divorce papers say, if either person's circumstances alter "substantially," the court may change or end alimony.

The Internal Revenue Code requires that the court papers state that alimony ends when the recipient dies. Other terms of the agreement or order may determine whether or not alimony is reviewed or ends if:

- the recipient lives with a "significant other,"
- the recipient has a roommate,
- the recipient receives substantial support from another,
- the recipient remarries, or
- the person paying retires.

It is good to deal with the issues of live-in relationships, remarriage, and retirement in the agreement or order. (Agreements often contain more details than orders.) None of these events automatically ends alimony in New Hampshire. Most agreements specify a period of living together (maybe thirty, or sixty days) as a basis for ending alimony. In most cases, remarriage ends alimony, but there are situations where some other agreement would be reasonable. If all retirement plans are divided as part of the divorce, it may be fair to end alimony at retirement.

Changes in alimony after divorce

In New Hampshire, the court can review the issue of alimony at any time after the divorce. This happens when either former spouse files court papers to enforce or change the original agreement or order. (See chapter 16 on "After Divorce" for more information.)

If the person required to pay alimony either fails to pay or falls behind in the payments, and an "arrearage" (unpaid amount) builds up, the person who is supposed to receive the alimony may file a petition or a motion for contempt in order to force payment.

Either person may reopen the divorce case to modify the alimony order. He or she may ask to:

- increase or decrease the amount of alimony,
- extend alimony that has stopped or is due to stop,
- end alimony,
- resume alimony that has ended, so long as the request is within five years, or
- begin alimony for the first time, so long as the request is within five years of the divorce.

The general rule for modifying the order after the divorce is an "unforeseeable, substantial change in circumstances." Even if the parties have agreed in a premarital agreement or divorce agreement that there will never be alimony, the court may still decide to order it if the "need and ability to pay" test discussed earlier is met.

My spouse provides my health insurance through employment. How will I have insurance after the divorce?

This is a very technical area. It is best to get something in writing from your spouse's employer as well as legal advice. The employer can provide information on what coverage is available and the cost, if any. A lawyer can explain the applicable laws, including the New Hampshire law effective in 2008.

The permanent agreement may require your spouse to cooperate in maintaining your insurance after the divorce. This may be done under a federal law (COBRA) or a state law of New Hampshire, Massachusetts, or whatever state the employer is located in. Most New Hampshire employers are required to allow former spouses to stay on health insurance, without an additional premium. Depending on the choice of law and the employer's policies, there may or may not be a cost. The divorce agreement should say who will pay this cost, and, if paid by your spouse, whether the payment will be considered alimony.

The choice of law must be made promptly. Under the COBRA option, the employer must be notified within 30 days after the divorce and any premium paid promptly. You may lose the right to coverage if the deadlines are not met. Under COBRA, coverage is for a maximum of three years.

property division

13

Chapter 13

Property Division

UNDER NEW HAMPSHIRE LAW, ALL assets belonging to either or both spouses are considered "*marital property.*" Therefore, property or asset division is a central issue in most divorces. Property held or titled in one spouse's name may be divided or given to the other spouse. Even an asset owned before the marriage, or received as a gift or inheritance, is marital property and may be divided.

"Property," in the sense used in divorce, refers to everything of value, including: real estate, household contents, vehicles, bank accounts, stocks and bonds, business interests, pension and other retirement benefits (even if not yet vested), trusts, royalties, and copyrights.

How is property divided in New Hampshire?

If you and your spouse reach a stipulation or agreement, the court will generally approve your agreed-upon property division. Over 80 percent of divorcing couples work out an agreement on property division. However, if the court decides how to divide the property, because no agreement is possible, the court will apply the legal principles described below.

New Hampshire law requires that the property division be *equitable* (fair). What is equitable depends on the family situation. The law *presumes* that it is equitable for each spouse to get 50 percent of the property. This is what happens in most divorces, especially if the marriage lasted ten years or more. Note that each asset or item of property need not be divided equally; instead the total value of all property is divided. The amount of debt is usually a factor in property division.

Property division is decided only once, and is final, at the time of divorce. Unlike the decisions in parenting, child support, and alimony, the court may not later modify the property division! (Exceptions are rare, and must be based upon fraud or similar reasons. See chapter 16 for specifics.)

What factors may justify an unequal division?

In some cases, a property division in which each spouse receives 50 percent may not be "equitable." The division may instead be 45/55, 40/60, or some other ratio. New Hampshire law specifies fifteen factors to be considered in evaluating whether a 50/50 division would be fair:

1. The length of the marriage
2. The age, health, social or economic status, occupation, vocational skills, employability, separate property, amount and sources of income, needs, and liabilities (debts) of each spouse
3. The opportunity of each spouse to acquire capital assets and income in the future
4. If there is a minor child, the ability of a care-taking parent to be employed without substantially interfering with the interests of the child
5. If there is a minor child, the need of a care-taking parent to occupy or own the family home and to use or own the household contents

6. The contribution of either spouse to the growth or the reduction in value of the property

7. Significant differences between the spouses in their contributions to the marriage, including contributions to the care and education of the child and the care and management of the home

8. Any contribution made by one spouse to help educate or develop the career of the other, or any interruption of either spouse's educational or personal career opportunities for the benefit of the other's career or the marriage or the child

9. Pension or retirement rights earned before or during the marriage

10. The tax consequences

11. The value of property covered by a valid premarital contract

12. The fault of either party, if it caused the marriage to break down

13. The value of any premarital property

14. The value of any property acquired by gift or inheritance

15. Any other factor that the court considers relevant

How does "fault" affect property division?

Most New Hampshire divorces are "no-fault" divorces, based, technically, on "irreconcilable differences." However, the law also allows divorce based on *fault*, or the bad behavior of one spouse. Some grounds for a fault divorce are: adultery (sexual intercourse with a person of the opposite sex other than your spouse), extreme cruelty, and "conduct so as to endanger health and reason." The spouse asking for a divorce based on fault must be innocent of fault. If both are guilty, the faults balance each other. (See chapter 1 for more information on fault and no-fault divorce.)

If the marriage breakdown is due to fault, the court may award the innocent spouse more than half the assets. In New Hampshire, for fault to be considered by the court, the "fault" must meet the following two-part test:

- The fault has caused the breakdown of the marriage; *and*
- the fault must have either:
  — caused substantial physical or mental pain and suffering to the innocent spouse; or
  — caused substantial economic loss.

In some of these cases, even if the innocent spouse proves that fault caused the breakdown of the marriage, this factor may make little or no difference in the property division. Instead of 50 percent, the innocent spouse may get 52 or 55 percent; or the split may still be 50/50.

In some cases, the court decides that the fault existed, but that it was not the cause of the breakdown. For example, the court decides that the marriage broke down before the adultery happened. In others cases, the court decides that the fault caused the breakdown, but the second part of the test (substantial harm or economic loss) was not met. For example, the court might decide that the innocent spouse didn't suffer enough for the fault to count. In these situations, the two-part test has not been met, and the innocent spouse gets no additional property because of fault.

Introducing fault into a case usually prolongs the case and increases costs. It can also make co-parenting difficult. In deciding whether to put fault in your court papers, consider the advantages and disadvantages. Ask your lawyer about your options.

Length of marriage

If the marriage was short and without children, the usual goal of property division is simply to get each spouse back to the financial position he or she had at the time of the marriage. In long marriages, say over ten years, in which the only substantial asset is the family home, the assets are usually split 50/50. The longer the marriage, the more likely that the division will be 50/50.

Other common factors

Several of the fifteen property division factors usually favor a spouse who stayed at home or worked only part-time because of a child. If one spouse owned the property before the marriage or inherited it recently, the "owner" usually gets most of this property. However, if the marriage is long or the asset has been treated as joint property, the source of the property is not considered important and the assets may be divided equally.

How will our marital property be divided?

The legal principles discussed above do not determine the specifics of how a couple's assets will be divided. As most property is divided by agreement, the divorcing couple may chose to ignore some or most of the principles.

Property may be divided asset by asset (each spouse getting 50 percent of each item); or an asset given to only one of the spouses may be balanced against an asset going to the other spouse. Usually a combination of these two methods is used. Some items go to each spouse and others are divided, or are sold and the proceeds are divided.

Sometimes, one spouse receives all of a valuable asset and then makes payments to the other over time as reimbursement. The agreement or order may give the person who is to receive the payments a mortgage or a security interest in the asset (or in another asset), to insure payment. The payment over time is often used for a family home or a small business. Another plan for the home is to agree to sell it in the future and divide the proceeds as of the time of sale. The future date may be a set number of years ("within three years") or a child-related deadline ("when the youngest finishes high school").

How are different types of retirement plans handled?

All types of retirement accounts and benefits are marital property in New Hampshire. They are divided under the same equitable standard as other assets. Retirement benefits can be divided into two categories, defined benefit plans and defined contribution plans:

• *Defined benefit plans:* These are traditional pensions; the employee has the right to receive certain benefits at retirement. The benefits are generally based on a formula tied to salary or wages during the final years of employment. In this type of retirement plan, there is no specific individual account in the employee's name. Instead, there is money held in a general pension fund for all employees, which may include employee contributions. Military retirement plans and certain other government plans are included in this category, even though they are funded differently from private plans.

The value of a defined benefit plan is more than the total of contributions to date. It includes the value of the right to receive payments in the future, as set out in the plan. To find out the value of a defined benefit plan, it must be appraised (valued).

There are several ways to do this: use a computerized pension-appraisal service, hire a pension actuary or a CPA, or use computer software. (See the "Resources" list in appendix C for computerized services.)

• *Defined contribution plans:* These include 401(k)s, profit-sharing, thrift-savings, employee stock ownership plans, and IRAs. Each employee has a separate account, the value of which is listed on periodic statements from the plan or financial institution.

Generally, there is little problem in obtaining a value for defined contribution plans, as the plan administrator provides statements on an annual or more frequent basis. No appraisals are needed. If the plan is an individually-controlled IRA, the bank or financial institution can provide the statement.

Funds in defined contribution plans are not available to the employee or IRA owner without payment of taxes and penalties. However, the entire amount or a portion of it may be rolled over into an IRA or other retirement plan belonging to the spouse, by means of a special court order called a QDRO (see below) or a similar order. A few plans require the non-employee spouse to keep his or her portion in a separate account in the plan until retirement. Some defined contribution plans may be borrowed against to get cash to buy out the other spouse's interest.

How are retirement plans divided?

For many spouses, the need to divide retirement accounts is a sensitive issue. The spouse may say: "I worked for it, so I should get it all." Or, "I can't get my retirement for many years, until I'm 65, so my spouse shouldn't get anything."

Because New Hampshire law treats retirement benefits the same as other assets, they must be included in property division. If there are several retirement plans, perhaps some in the name of each spouse, they may be viewed as a category of assets. Then, all the retirement benefits are added up and divided 50/50 and all the non-retirement assets are added up and divided 50/50. Some couples agree that one spouse will get all the retirement assets while the other spouse receives the house or other assets. (See the discussion in chapter 3 of asset-tradeoffs.)

If the plan is a defined benefit one, the spouse will get his or her share at retirement age. (Defined benefit plans rarely permit lump sum distributions prior to retirement.) If the plan is a defined contribution, the spouse's share may be put in a separate account or rolled into an IRA. There is no tax or penalty due when retirement benefits are properly divided at divorce. However, if either spouse withdraws funds before retirement, that spouse will owe both tax and penalties.

Defined benefit plans may be divided in two ways:

- Determine the value, and either offset it against another asset or have the employee buy out the other spouse's interest.
- Divide the pension itself by means of a QDRO (special court order). There are two methods of doing this:
  — Shared payment when employee receives benefit; former spouse gets a percentage
  — Separate interest; this divides the benefit into two separate annuities

In one respect, the New Hampshire law on dividing defined benefit plans is different than the law for other property. Generally, defined benefit plans are divided based on the pension's value on the date when the petition requesting divorce was filed at court. Other dates are often used for other types of property.

Depending upon how you intend to divide the pension, you may or may not need valuation. If it is going to be divided by the *coverture fraction* (in New Hampshire called the *Hodgins formula*) the spouse simply receives his or her portion when the benefits are payable at retirement. The portion that the non-employee spouse will receive is described by a formula. The key to understanding the formula is the concept of *coverture*, which is the period or portion of the pension the spouse is entitled to share in. (In New Hampshire, coverture is the period of marriage up to the filing of the petition for divorce.)

The formula divides the coverture period by the total period of employment:

$$\frac{\text{Coverture period}}{\text{Total period of employment}} \times 50\%$$

The result is the portion of each monthly pension benefit that the non-employee spouse would receive. If the employed spouse continues to work for the same employer, the ratio of the coverture period to the total employment goes down. If the formula is being used, it should be spelled out both in the permanent agreement or the proposed orders and in a separate QDRO.

What are QDROs?

Dividing many retirement plans requires an additional court document. For private employer plans, this court paper is called a Qualified Domestic Relations Order. This is usually abbreviated as QDRO (pronounced "quad-row"). The QDRO is a special court order which is sent to the plan administrator, the person legally responsible for the particular retirement plan. The QDRO authorizes paying out portions of the plan to a spouse or former spouse.

For dividing federal government retirement accounts (both civilian and military), the special court document has other names. An IRA does not require a QDRO.

Except for IRAs, valuing and dividing retirement benefits is one of the most technical parts of a divorce. It is important to get legal and tax advice before making decisions in this area. (See chapter 14 on "Taxes and Divorce" for more information.)

Summary of steps to divide property

In summary, these are the basic steps that should be taken to divide property:

- Make a careful list of all assets owned jointly.
- Make a careful list of all assets owned by one spouse, including any owned jointly with someone else.
- Value each asset. For bank accounts, mutual funds, 401(k)s, and similar assets, this means getting a current statement.
- If there is any debt against the asset, get a current balance.
- Divide the house contents by agreement.
- Sell any assets that neither spouse wants.
- Make a fair division of the house, other real estate, retirement benefits, investments, business interests, and other property.
- Complete the paperwork that is needed to change from joint names to one spouse's name, or to otherwise carry out the property division.

∞

taxes
and
divorce

14

Chapter 14

Taxes and Divorce

by Hollis McGuire, MBA, CPA
(Updated by Timothy R. Hepburn, CPA, MBA)

Why should I care about taxes?

TAX LAW IS COMPLICATED. You probably don't like to think about it except right before April 15. However, there are aspects to a divorce that can have important tax ramifications. Making the right decisions might mean hundreds or thousands of dollars to you. You must either learn *enough* about taxes and divorce to make good choices, or you must get advice from a CPA or a tax attorney. Best of all is to do both.

The Internal Revenue Service has information to help you with these decisions. See the "Resources" section in appendix C for details on contacting the Internal Revenue Service. You may also refer to appendix A, "More Tax Tips," for a further discussion of taxes.

What are the tax issues during and after a divorce?

Some of the areas of concern that relate to taxes during a divorce are:

- Filing status
- Exemptions
- Deductions and credits

- Joint or separate returns
- Alimony
- Educational incentives
- Property division
- Retirement plans and QDROs
- State taxes

Unless you have had a short marriage with no children, it is very likely that many of these concerns apply to your divorce. Each of these concerns is discussed in this chapter. Only some of the divorce tax issues apply in civil unions. Get advice from a lawyer or CPA.

What filing status should I use during the divorce?

Your marital status on the *last* day of your tax-filing year determines the options available to you for your filing category on your tax return. If you are legally married, you have certain choices; if you are divorced, you have others. If you were still legally married on December 31 (even if you become divorced before you file your tax return), you must file for that tax year as one of the following:

- Married, filing jointly
- Married, filing separately
- Head of household

Generally, the court will not order divorcing spouses to file jointly. If your spouse does not agree to file jointly, you will not have that option anyway. You and your spouse can agree to file jointly, and this usually results in the lowest total tax. It is also possible to amend a separate filing to a joint one at a later date, if you eventually reach agreement on this. However, once a joint return is filed, it cannot be amended to two separate returns.

Although, under current law, you will probably pay more in taxes if you choose to file as "married filing separately," this will ensure that you will not be liable for your spouse's tax debts. If you file as "head of household" you will also not be liable for your spouse's tax debts, but there are certain criteria you must meet to do this. (These are described in a later section of this chapter.) If you want payments from one spouse to another to be tax-deductible alimony, you must file separate returns.

What filing status should I use after the divorce?

If your divorce is final on or before December 31, you must file either as "single" or as "head of household." You may no longer file as "married." If you have obtained a final decree of legal separation by the end of the year, you are also considered unmarried for that year.

If you and your spouse are working out the divorce decisions informally, in mediation, or through negotiation, you may be able to arrange the timing of the divorce to your advantage. For example, you could reach an agreement in October that the divorce will take effect in January. It is important to get legal advice about the pros and cons of such a decision. (See chapter 4 on "How to Make Divorce Decisions.")

Can I file as "head of household?"

The tax burden for a "head of household" is less than for someone filing as "single" or as "married, filing separately." If you qualify to use this filing status, you can save a significant amount in taxes.

You can only file as "head of household" if you maintain a home for your unmarried child (or other relative who is your dependent) for more than six months during the year. In order to qualify as having maintained a home, the person must live with you (unless this is your parent) and you must be providing for more than one-half of the cost of the home.

"Costs of the home" included in this calculation are rent, property tax, mortgage interest, maintenance, utilities, food eaten in the home, home insurance, and household expenses, such as repairs. If you pay for these things, even if you use money you have received as child support or alimony, it counts as part of the costs of the home. If you are still married as of December 31, there is an additional requirement: you must not have lived with your spouse in the last six months of the year.

You can file as "head of household" if you meet the requirements above, even though the other parent is claiming the dependency exemption for your child. For some families, a fair arrangement may be for one parent to use "head of household" status, and the other to receive the exemption.

What is the difference between deductions, exemptions, and credits?

A *deduction* is an amount subtracted from your income, reducing the amount of income that will be taxed. An *exemption* is a deduction of a set amount for each qualifying person. A *credit* is an amount subtracted from your tax obligation.

How do deductions work?

Deductions reduce your tax bill by reducing your taxable income. Each tax return filed contains either standard or itemized deductions. The filer chooses between standard and *itemized deductions* depending on which gives a better (lower tax) result.

The *standard deduction* is a set amount for each taxpayer. Check with a CPA or the IRS for current amounts. For 2007, the standard deductions are:

- Single: $5,350
- Married, filing separately: $5,350
- Head of household: $7,850
- Married, filing jointly: $10,700

The total amount the standard deduction will reduce your taxes will depend upon your tax bracket. Itemized deductions are based on actual expenses that you have paid that qualify as deductions. They may or may not provide bigger tax savings than the standard deduction. (See appendix A for further discussion on deductions.)

Deductions have several additional complications. Many deductions are subject to income limits. These can reduce the value of a deduction, especially for high-income taxpayers.

How do exemptions work?

You get one exemption for yourself (and one for your spouse if filing jointly). For each dependent (such as a child) you get an additional exemption, as long as the divorce agreement does not allocate the dependent exemption to the other parent. For 2007, each exemption has been set at $3,400. The amount that each exemption reduces your tax depends on your tax bracket. For example:

- 15 percent tax bracket = $510 tax reduction
- 28 percent tax bracket = $952 tax reduction
- 35 percent tax bracket = $1,190 tax reduction

Check with the IRS or your accountant for the amount of each exemption in your current year.

Which parent gets the exemption for our child?

Federal law gives the exemption to the parent with whom the child lived for more than half of the year, even if the other parent pays for more than 50 percent of the child's support. However, the exemption may be *transferred* to the other parent. The parent with whom the child lives for more than half the year can waive (give up) his or her right to the exemption by signing Internal Revenue Service Form 8332 and sending it to the other parent. If you and your spouse do not agree about who should get the exemption, the court has the authority to decide.

The divorce agreement or order may state who gets the exemption, and if and when Form 8332 will be provided, along with any other conditions the paying parent must meet to get the exemption. However, if the agreement or order does not mention the exemption, the parent with whom the child lives for more than half the year gets the exemption. For further information regarding exemptions for dependents, please see appendix A and IRS Publication 501.

The parent with whom the child lived for more than half of the year can waive the right for one year, or for all future years, or for anything in between. The exemption may be alternated, with one parent having even-numbered years and the other having odd-numbered years.

If the exemption is transferred, the parent with whom the child lives for less than half the year attaches Form 8332 to his or her tax return. If the form is for multiple years, the parent files the original with the first year's return, and sends a copy of the form with each future year's return.

Once the exemption is given up for future years, this decision cannot be undone. Because circumstances can change, you may decide to fill in Form 8332 for the current year only. On the other hand, many divorcing spouses want as many issues as possible decided finally, to avoid further disputes. You should weigh these alternatives and ask your lawyer and accountant for advice.

The "head of household" status often creates better tax savings than the dependency exemption. The tax rates for "head of household" are lower than the rates for single individuals, and the standard deduction is higher. This tax status can result in tax savings which could amount to more than $1,000, and sometimes more than $2,000. (See the discussion earlier in this chapter to see if you qualify for a "head of household" filing status.)

What happens if we have two or more children, or have equal periods of residential responsibility?

If you and your spouse have two or more children:

- you may each get one or more exemptions, or
- the exemptions may go together to one parent.

You may both be entitled to claim "head of household," if each meets the requirement for one child. Check with your CPA about your options.

If you have equal periods of residential responsibility, the agreement or orders should state how the exemptions will be divided. As both of you have a child living with you half of the time, one or both of you should complete a Form 8332. This will make it clear who is legally entitled to the exemption in a specific year.

Note that if both parents collectively do not provide more than half of the child's support, or if the child lived with someone other than a parent for more than six months, *neither* parent can claim the exemption. (See appendix A for details on the IRS test for dependency.)

Am I eligible for a tax credit?

Credits are dollar-for-dollar direct reductions in the tax you would otherwise pay. Therefore, credits can be much more valuable than deductions or exemptions. However, credits can also be subject to limits, especially for high-income earners. Examples of credits are the Child Tax Credit, the Credit for Child and Dependent Care Expenses, and the Hope Scholarship Credit (see below).

What is the child tax credit?

The child tax credit originated with the 1997 Taxpayer Relief Act. For 2007, you can take a credit of up to $1,000 for each child under age seventeen by December 31. Because the credit is subtracted from your total tax, the value of the credit is the full $1,000.

Note that this credit is limited by the income of the parent or parents, depending on your filing status. The credit starts to phase out at $75,000 for single filers, $110,000 for joint filers, and $55,000 for married filing separately, based on modified, adjusted gross income. The IRS instruction booklet for Form 1040 and IRS Publication 972 have more information on this credit.

What are child care credits and dependent care reimbursements?

Parents with a child under age thirteen are eligible for a credit for child care expenses. This is available if the child care is required to allow the parent to earn income, or to be a full-time student, or if the parent is disabled. Only the parent with whom the child lives for more than half the year is eligible for the credit. Only expenses paid by that parent qualify. For most families, it is generally best for the parent with whom the child lived for more than half of the year to pay the child care costs directly. IRS Publication 503, "Child and Dependent Care Expenses," provides detailed information and examples to complete IRS Form 2441 to claim the credit. (See chapter 11 on "Child Support" for information on how child care expenses may affect the amount of child support.)

A *dependent care reimbursement account* is a benefit offered by an employer. It allows an employee to designate wages into a special account for dependent care, and those wages are exempt from income tax. Only the parent with whom the child lives for more than half the year can make use of a dependent care reimbursement account.

What are "educational" tax incentives?

Educational incentives include the Hope Scholarship Tax Credit, the Lifetime Learning Credit, Coverdell Education savings account (previously known as educational IRAs), the deduction for student loan interest, and qualified tuition and fees. Only the parent who receives the dependency exemption may qualify to take these credits and deductions for the child's educational expenses. However, either parent may take either the Hope Scholarship or Lifetime Learning Credit for the parent's *own* qualifying educational expenses. (For details on these incentives, see appendix A.)

What happens if I sign a joint return and my spouse has lied on it?

If your spouse has lied on a tax return, the first step is to get advice from a CPA or tax attorney. If you can qualify as an "innocent spouse," you will not be liable for debts which are connected to your spouse. In 1998, innocent spouse relief was expanded. The understatement of tax no longer needs to be either substantial or grossly erroneous (it can be less than $500 in tax). If you knew of an understatement but not the extent of the understatement, you may be held liable for only the portion of understatement actually known.

If you are still married to your spouse and chose to file a joint return, you may still elect innocent spouse relief within two years from the date of the first collection activity. At the time of the election, you must either be divorced, have lived apart for one year, or have obtained a legal separation. The new laws apply in full for tax liabilities that arise after July 1998, as well as to prior liabilities not yet paid as of that date.

To be an "innocent spouse," you must file IRS Form 8857 electing to take advantage of the law. Consult a CPA or tax attorney about when to file and what years to file for. Also see IRS Publication 971 on "Innocent Spouse Relief."

How is alimony treated for tax purposes?

Alimony is a payment made from one spouse or former spouse to the other, under a court order or written agreement approved by the court. The document may either be temporary or permanent. (See chapter 11 on "Alimony" for details on other, non-tax aspects of alimony.)

Alimony is generally taxable income. The person who receives the alimony claims it as income and the person who pays the alimony deducts it from income. Usually the recipient will need to increase withholding from employment income or make quarterly estimated payments. Don't wait until you sign your tax return to consider this!

Alimony is entered on the Internal Revenue Service Tax Return (Form 1040). The person paying alimony lists it as a deduction, and gives the recipient's Social Security number. The recipient lists it as income.

The federal requirements for payments to be considered alimony are as follows:

- The payments must be in cash (including check or money orders payable on demand).

- Payments must be received under a "divorce or separate maintenance instrument." This means either an order or an agreement approved by the court.

- The payment must be made either directly to a spouse or former spouse, or to a third party on behalf of the spouse.

- The agreement or order does not say that the payment is not alimony.

- If the payments are made under a final divorce agreement or order, the paying spouse and the recipient must not be members of the same household at the time the payment is made. However, this requirement may not apply if the payment is for temporary alimony prior to the divorce.

- There must be no requirement to make any payment, or a substitute for such payment, after the death of the recipient.

- The payments must not be for child support.

- If the spouses are still legally married to each other, they must not file a joint tax return. (There may be a joint return with a new spouse.)

Is alimony always taxable and deductible?

For tax purposes, alimony designated as non-taxable is no longer considered to be alimony, and is generally considered to be a property settlement. You can designate alimony payments as non-taxable (and non-deductible), but this must be spelled out in your divorce agreement. The person paying alimony will not get a deduction. The recipient will not report it as income. However, since alimony is usually paid by a person in a higher tax bracket and received by a person in a lower tax bracket, such an agreement is rare. Taxable alimony can often be structured to result in overall tax savings to the family.

The agreement or order does not need to state that a payment is alimony if it meets the legal requirements. However, it makes it clearer to everyone, if the agreement or order does state that it is alimony!

Can paying mortgage or other house expenses qualify as "alimony?"

Frequently, the spouse or former spouse who has moved out of the house is paying the mortgage or other house expenses. Whether such expenses can be considered alimony follows some special and fairly complicated rules. (See appendix A for more information.) It is best to consult a CPA or tax attorney for advice on how the rules would apply to you.

What payments to a spouse or former spouse are not alimony?

Payments made voluntarily, before a court order or court approval of a written agreement, are not alimony for tax purposes. Payments made that exceed the amount required by the written agreement or order are not alimony. If the former spouses are living together even after a divorce or legal separation is made final, any payments made will not be taxable or deductible as alimony. Child support is not alimony either.

Alimony ends upon the death of the recipient and the

divorce agreement or order must state this. If payments to a former spouse must continue to be paid after his or her death, none of the payments either before or after death will qualify as alimony. An example of a disqualifying provision is a requirement to pay a lump sum to the estate of the former spouse. (See appendix A for some examples of when alimony is not deductible or taxable.)

Can I pay more alimony instead of child support, and get a tax break?

Child support payments are determined by state rules. The payment amount is affected by the number of children, income, and certain expenses. There are different rules for reviewing or ending child support. For all these reasons, you cannot convert child support to alimony for a tax break. The law prevents this by prohibiting alimony payments that are structured to end on dates that coincide with a child reaching age eighteen or twenty-one.

What if alimony is not paid or the amount changes?

If you have a court order requiring alimony, but you do not receive it, do not report this as alimony. If alimony payments are in arrears and a lump sum payment is made to catch up with the order, this should generally be reported as alimony. The same principle applies if you are the paying person. If you don't actually pay, you may not take the deduction.

If alimony payments are not made in a timely fashion, or there was a reduction or termination of payment during the first three calendar years of the divorce, IRS recapture rules might apply. Recapture happens when the IRS determines that payment claimed as alimony was not alimony, and requires payment of taxes and penalties. The rules are complicated. (See appendix A for an outline.) For specific advice in your case, you should consult your accountant or tax attorney.

Is there tax on alimony in New Hampshire?

Alimony is neither taxable income nor reportable income for purposes of New Hampshire taxes.

Is child support taxable and deductible?

Amounts paid to support a child are non-deductible. Therefore, child support is not reported on tax returns as either a deduction or as income. In order to be considered "child support," the divorce decree must have fixed the amount of support, the payment must be for the support of the payer's children, and the order must be in effect when the payments are made. In New Hampshire, both temporary and final orders require child support amounts to be specified.

Will property division affect my taxes?

As part of the property division, assets may be changed from joint names to one spouse's name; or all or part of an asset in one spouse's name may be given to the other spouse. For tax purposes, these changes in ownership are called "transfers." See chapter 13 for a discussion of other aspects of property division.

When an asset (such as a bank account, brokerage account, home, retirement account, or furnishings) is transferred "incident to a divorce," no taxable income or expense is created. The asset transfer does not get reported on a federal tax return or on any New Hampshire tax return.

Can we avoid taxes and penalties when dividing the retirement benefits?

Dividing the rights to retirement plans of an employed spouse will not result in any taxes or penalties when the transfers are done properly and they continue to be held for retirement. Dividing retirement savings that are in a qualified retirement plan is done by a Qualified Domestic Relations Order (QDRO). A QDRO gives a spouse, former spouse, or child specified rights to a retirement plan.

Dividing an IRA is even simpler. The bank or other financial institution will divide the account if the divorce agreement or order requires it. Unless there is a withdrawal, there will not be any taxes or penalties attached to this.

What if part of the property division is delayed for several years after the divorce?

When a transfer of property is related to the ending of the marriage and it occurs within one year of the effective date of the divorce, federal tax law classifies it as "incident to the divorce." Transfers of property that occur between two and six years after the divorce are classified as "incident to the divorce" only if the transfers are part of the final divorce order.

Transfers that take place after the sixth anniversary of the divorce are presumed to be unrelated to the divorce. However, these transfers can be classified as "incident to the divorce" if the transfer was directly related to division of property owned by the spouses at the time of the divorce. (See appendix A for more information on tax issues relating to property division.)

Are the costs of divorce deductible?

Legal fees and court costs are generally not deductible expenses. However, fees paid for tax advice, or fees paid that relate to obtaining alimony (which will result in taxable income) may be deductible if certain legal requirements are met and you itemize expenses. These fees are considered "miscellaneous deductions." They are only of benefit if the miscellaneous deductions are greater than 2 percent of your adjusted gross income. Therefore, even if you have deductible expenses, there may be no tax savings involved. Talk to your CPA or tax attorney.

What other steps are necessary to put my federal income taxes in order?

Here are five other things you will need to take care of:

1. Visit your local IRS office, or the Internal Revenue Service's web site (**www.irs.gov**) to obtain Internal Revenue Service Publication 504, "Tax Information for Divorced or Separated Individuals." It will provide valuable information on a variety of tax topics related to your divorce.

2. Review your estimated tax obligations during the year of the divorce, preferably with an accountant or tax attorney. For example, if you sell assets or receive alimony during the year, this may cause tax payments to be due, and can create a quarterly obligation to file estimated taxes. If you wait until you need to file the return, you may owe interest and penalties on underpayment, as well as a significant tax payment.

3. Recalculate your withholding status at work. Obtain a new W-4 (Employee's Withholding Allowance Certificate) from your employer. You can submit an updated W-4 at any time during the year. The Internal Revenue Service web site (**www.irs.gov**) has a withholding calculator.

4. If you move, notify the Internal Revenue Service of your new address by filing Form 8822 as soon as you move.

5. If you are changing your name, notify the Social Security Administration (SSA). The name you use to file your tax return must agree with the name Social Security has on file. File Form SS-5 at a local SSA office to change your name. The form is available on the agency's web site, www.socialsecurity.gov or by calling (800) 772-1213.

What is the impact of divorce on New Hampshire state taxes?

Although divorce always has both short-term and long-term federal tax consequences, only rarely does it impact New Hampshire state taxes. The two possible areas of concern are interest and dividends income, and business income. (See appendix A for an outline of these issues.) Changes in New Hampshire tax structure could make state taxes more important in divorce. Check with your accountant.

Final thoughts

This overview of tax-related issues during divorce may not address every issue you will encounter. Appendix A has other information and more tax tips. Remember that federal and state tax laws are revised and reinterpreted on a continuing basis. You should consult with an advisor who specializes in this area for advice on your particular situation.

∞

appeals

15

Chapter 15

Appeals

What court handles appeals?

AN *APPEAL* IS A REQUEST to a higher-level court to change or throw out a court decision. New Hampshire has a Supreme Court consisting of a Chief Justice and four Associate Justices. It is the only appellate (appeals) court in the New Hampshire state court system. The Supreme Court considers appeals from the District, Superior, Family Division, and Probate Courts, and from certain administrative agencies. The Court is also responsible for:

- The ethical rules for attorneys and judges
- The discipline of attorneys and judges
- The procedural rules and forms for state courts
- The general administration of all state courts

There is a separate federal court system, including the Federal District Court in Concord, the First Circuit Court of Appeals in Boston and the United States Supreme Court in Washington, DC. Generally, the federal courts do not deal with divorce. Of the hundreds of divorces I have handled, only two were taken to federal court. One concerned military issues and the other an international child abduction.

I don't like my divorce agreement or orders. Will an appeal fix them?

Not likely! Very few cases are appealed. Most civil cases

(including divorce and other family law cases) are settled by an agreement signed by the parties. *Settled* cases cannot be appealed. If you sign an agreement with the other side, you may not appeal. Only a *contested* issue decided by a master or judge may be appealed. The basis for an appeal is one or more of the following:

- The master or judge made a mistake in interpreting the law.
- The master or judge made a mistake in applying the law to the facts of the case.
- The master or judge has gone beyond his or her allowable discretion.
- The master or judge has made findings that are not supported by the evidence.

In a divorce or other civil matter, a claim that your lawyer did a poor job presenting your case is not grounds for an appeal.

Preparing and handling an appeal is a technical area of the law. Some appeals are handled by the lawyer who represented the person in the Family Division. In other cases, a specialist in appellate work either prepares the appeal or assists the original lawyer. Either way, an appeal will add many thousands of dollars to your legal bill.

When do appeals happen?

Most cases are presented to the Supreme Court after there has been a final decision "on the merits" in the lower court or administrative agency. In rare situations, the court accepts an *interlocutory appeal*, a transfer of a question arising during a case pending in a lower court.

Important steps before an appeal

If a case *may* be appealed, certain things must be done before and during the hearing in the Family Division. It is important to have a *record* of this hearing. This means that a court monitor or stenographer takes down every word said, either in shorthand or by tape recorder. The act of taking down the proceedings is "making a record." If the case is appealed, the appealing party is responsible for providing the Supreme Court with the record necessary to decide the appeal. Typically this means paying the costs of having what was said at the trial or motion hearing typed into a transcript.

At the Family Division hearing, the lawyer usually submits certain documents to aid the master or judge in making his or her decision. If later there is an appeal, these same documents, and the trial court's response to them, will help the Supreme Court understand what happened in the lower court. These documents may include a proposed order, requests for findings of fact, and requests for rulings of law.

The requests for findings are especially important. These are legally significant facts about the case, put into a logical order to aid the court in deciding the case in one party's favor. As part of a written decision, the master or judge will "find" certain facts to be true.

What are the steps to appeal a divorce decision?

There are specific requirements and timetables for an appeal, according to the type of case. As an illustration, I will describe a typical appeal of a final divorce order. The Family Division issues the decision in a contested divorce approximately one to three months after the hearing. When the decision is issued, it comes with a notice of decision from the clerk. The notice states an effective date, which is thirty days from the date on the clerk's notice of decision.

Within ten days of the notice of decision, either side may file a motion to reconsider, to allow the master or judge to correct errors that are claimed. Unless the master or judge has made an obvious error in the facts or has failed to make orders about one of the issues in the case, the motion to reconsider is usually denied. The decision to appeal to the New Hampshire Supreme Court must be made quickly, as the court documents must be filed within thirty days of the notice of decision on the motion to reconsider. An appeal may also be filed directly after the final decision, *without* filing a motion to reconsider. In this situation, the deadline is thirty days after the notice of decision.

The first document in the appeal is called a *notice of appeal*. The Supreme Court Rules supply the form that must be followed. The form must be filled out completely and the original and eight copies filed with the Supreme Court by the thirty-day deadline. The notice of appeal contains clerical information about the case, the list of the issues being appealed, and a transcript order notice. The relevant court documents from the case are attached to the notice of appeal. There is a filing fee.

What happens in an appeal?

A New Hampshire appeal has several stages. First, the court issues a deadline by which the appealing party must pay the lower court for the transcript production. The Court will not issue a briefing schedule until the transcript is completed. Once the transcript is completed the appealing party is given 30-45 days to submit his/her brief and the opposing party is given a similar deadline after the receipt of the opening brief. The court issues a scheduling order, or on rare occasion, issues a prehearing evaluation conference order or a summary disposition order. A scheduling order gives the dates for important steps in the cases. The purpose of a prehearing evaluation conference is to consider the possibility of settlement, the simplification of issues, or other ways of more efficiently processing the case.

The Supreme Court has several methods of handling appeals.

The Supreme Court has several different ways of handling appeals: summary disposition order, memo decision, 3JX panel, published decision without oral argument, and published decision after oral argument before the full court.

What is a summary disposition order?

This is a short memo decision deciding the case after briefing. Such orders are rare and usually are based on some procedural defect.

What is a 3JX case?

Generally, these are cases where the law is clear and one party claims the trial judge or master made a mistake. Cases assigned to the 3JX docket receive five-minute oral arguments before a panel of three Supreme Court Justices. The decision of the three justices must be unanimous or the case is sent to the full five-member court. 3JX decisions are usually received more quickly than full-court decisions.

Can cases get settled after an appeal is filed?

Sometimes people are able to reach an agreement after an appeal is filed. The most likely time is after the notice of appeal and before people have spent thousands of dollars on the transcript and briefs. In rare cases, the Supreme Court helps by bringing both sides to the court for a prehearing evaluation conference conducted by a current or retired justice.

What is a brief?

A *brief* is, in essence, a long legal research paper. (Nothing "brief" about it!) It includes legal arguments, and a discussion of how legal principles apply to the facts. After the filing person's brief is in, the other side has thirty or forty-five days to file his or her brief. After both briefs are received, they are reviewed by a staff attorney, who makes a recommendation as to whether the case should be decided by memo decision or referred to a 3JX panel or full court. These recommendations are reviewed and voted upon by the Court as a whole.

What is an oral argument?

The *oral argument* is a hearing at the Supreme Court. Not all appeals include oral argument. If the court decides to schedule oral argument, the case is assigned either to a 3-judge panel (3JX), or the full five-justice court. Only the lawyers speak. It is a chance for each lawyer to explain why the lower court decision should be changed, thrown out, or upheld.

Oral arguments are generally held at the Supreme Court building in Concord. The schedules for the current and upcoming months are available on the court web site **www.state.nh.us/courts/supreme.htm**. During oral arguments, there are no witnesses giving testimony. Each lawyer has only fifteen minutes (five minutes for 3JX) to present his or her position. When the red light on the lectern appears, the lawyer must finish quickly.

The oral argument at the Supreme Court is a challenge for any lawyer. The Justices usually do not let the lawyer present a carefully prepared speech. Much of the time is taken up by the Justices interrupting the argument to ask questions. The lawyer must make anticipating and answering the questions the priority.

How long does it take to get the Supreme Court's decision?

Decisions in 3JX cases are usually issued within a month. Cases argued before the full court receive a published (precedent-setting) decision. It may be four or six months or more from the full court oral argument to the written decision. The decisions are posted on the court web site and mailed to counsel. In divorce cases, the Supreme Court may:

- uphold the divorce order,
- vacate (set aside) the order, thus canceling it,
- reverse the order and remand it (send it back) to the trial court for a new trial, or
- reverse and remand only certain issues within the trial court decree (this happens often).

If there is an appeal, when will the divorce become final?

Except in rare instances, the divorce does not take effect until the entire case is over. Even if only the division of the house contents is appealed, the whole case is on hold. This means that an appealed divorce may be delayed for a year or two after the original hearing date. If you are considering an appeal, consider the impact of such a delay on your life.

Usually the temporary orders remain in effect until the appeal is over. Either side, however, may ask the Family Division to clarify what should happen on day-to-day issues, such as child support, or the division of household contents.

∽

after
divorce

16

Chapter 16

After Divorce

Why would anyone want to deal with the legal system or court again after getting divorced?

THERE ARE THREE AFTER-DIVORCE SITUATIONS that could require it:

- Both parties agree that a change in the parenting plan or divorce decree is needed.

- One side wants the parenting plan or decree changed.

- One side is not obeying the court orders.

What can I do during the divorce to avoid future legal problems?

To avoid further legal problems after a divorce is completed, the time to begin is *during* the divorce. In working out the divorce agreement and parenting plan, try to take a realistic view of the coming years.

If you agree to something you know is unworkable, you will have problems after the divorce. Even if you are anxious to put the divorce behind you, take time to cover all-important issues. The divorce agreement and especially the parenting plan must include many details. (See chapter 4 on "How to Make Divorce Decisions" and chapter 3 on "Money and Divorce.")

How can I avoid further legal problems with my former spouse?

After the divorce, try to maintain a businesslike relationship with your former spouse. If both sides try to live up to the spirit and words of the court orders, problems can usually be avoided. I suggest keeping a copy of your parenting plan and divorce agreement or order available for reference. If you have questions about what the court order means, consult a lawyer.

Parenting plans need to be adjusted due to special events, new work schedules, and children getting older. Focus on your child's needs, not any negative feelings about the other parent. Remember the message of the child impact program: fighting is harmful to your child.

If some problem comes up, try to work with your former spouse to resolve it without resorting to the courts. Mediation is often easier after a divorce, because people feel less hurt and angry. Collaborative practice can work well, or see if the issue can be negotiated between the lawyers. Only if these efforts fail should the problem be taken to the court. (See chapter 4 for details on your decision-making options, including page 60 on parenting coordination.)

Will I have problems concerning child support?

Child support is a common source of problems. I recommend keeping a careful record of every payment made or received. Include the date and amount.

If you are *paying* support, pay by check, electronic transfer, or wage assignment and keep the canceled checks or pay stubs. Do not give cash. Do not give the check to your former spouse when you exchange the child. This can confuse the child. *Mail* the check.

If you are receiving support, do not ask for cash. Do not request payment when the child is present. Deposit the check in a bank account; do not simply cash it. Do this whether the check is from the other parent, the state, or from the other parent's employer. Deposit it by itself, not with your paycheck. Note in your check register that the deposit is a child-support payment. Or ask if the parent could use an electronic transfer.

What if there are problems with parenting the children?

The same principle of keeping records applies if you are having problems with the parenting plan. If your child lives with the other parent most of the time and your parenting periods are refused or canceled, keep a diary of your attempts to set up time with the child and a record of the response of the other parent. If the child lives with you most of the time, keep a diary of when the other parent has time with the child. If a parenting period is canceled (with or without notice), or the child is returned early or late, keep a record of this also. If you ever have to take legal action, such a diary will be helpful, by showing a pattern of problems.

Can my parenting plan, divorce agreement, or orders be changed?

People often want to change something about their divorce orders. However, under New Hampshire law, only certain parts of a divorce order may be changed. It is very difficult to change anything about the property division (who gets which assets). To get the court to change the *property division*, you would have to show that there was fraud or a similar major legal problem with the court order.

The court can change who is to *use* a particular asset. For example, if the court says that the mother may use the home until the youngest child is eighteen, and later the primary residence of the children is changed to the father, the court may also give the father the use of the home. However, the actual property division may not be changed, except by agreement. Such agreements are rare; I have seen only two or three in my years of practice.

The terms of the agreements or orders on the following issues *may* be changed:

- Decision-making responsibility for child
- The parenting schedule
- The child's primary residence (if any)
- Child support
- Alimony
- Use of assets

What do we do to change the agreements or orders?

Any agreed-upon change to an earlier agreement or order must be put into writing, signed by both parties, and filed with the court. You may use the uniform support order form to change support and the court's parenting plan form to change parenting. The written, signed document must be filed with the court and approved by the judge, except a one-time change such as where your child spends Christmas this year. Unless an ongoing change is filed with the court, the change is not "legal." If the change concerns child support or other financial issues, the court will also require the necessary financial forms. (See chapter 7 on "Court Papers.")

To arrive at an agreement, you have the same choices available as you had when you were facing the divorce: informal agreement, mediation, collaborative practice, negotiation through lawyers, and litigation in court. (See chapter 4.)

The parenting schedule often needs to be adjusted as

the children get older or if one parent moves out of the area. Usually an agreement is worked out informally or through mediation. If no agreement is possible, the court may appoint a guardian *ad litem*. (See chapter 10 for how contested parenting cases are handled.)

Can the child's "primary residence" be changed?

If a child lives with one parent most of the time, that home is sometimes called the child's primary residence. Unless there is an agreement, it is difficult to change the child's primary residence after a divorce or parenting case. Consider using mediation to work out this issue. Without an agreement, you must prove that the child's present environment is detrimental to his or her physical, mental, or emotional health and the advantage to the child of a change outweighs the harm likely caused by the change. This is a difficult test to meet.

If the parenting plan has an equal or approximately equal schedule, an easier test may apply. The best interest of the child test is used if both parents agree, or the court finds, that the schedule is not working.

There is also an easier test for teenagers. If a child is a "mature minor" (probably about thirteen or fourteen), the child's opinion about whom he or she wants to live with is given considerable weight. However, this does not apply if the child's choice is based on "improper influences."

If the parties cannot agree on a change in primary residence, the court may appoint a guardian *ad litem* to represent the child and investigate whether there should be a change. This is a time-consuming and expensive procedure. (See chapter 10 on parenting cases.) It is much easier to change decision-making responsibility or the parenting schedule. The legal tests are less strict for these issues.

What does it take to get the court to change child support?

Child support can be changed if it has been three years since your divorce or last support order; or it can be changed earlier based on a *substantial change* in circumstances. The substantial change can be on either side and must consist of major unexpected increases in expenses or increases or decreases in income. The earliest child support may be changed by the court is after a petition is filed and then "served" on the other parent.

Support in New Hampshire is based on a complicated formula, called the Guidelines. (See chapter 11 on "Child Support" for details, including "exceptions.") If support is changed, it will be based on the Guidelines formula, unless a special circumstance applies.

Can alimony be changed?

Alimony *can* be changed after the divorce; it may be extended for a longer period, or decreased or increased. The basic test for alimony is always the same: need and ability to pay: does one person have the ability to pay while the other person needs alimony? (See chapter 12 on "Alimony.")

When we were divorced, there was no alimony order. Can it be ordered now?

Alimony may also be ordered for the first time up to five years after the divorce, if the economic situation changes for the divorced parties. It is not necessary that alimony was part of the divorce. The test is "need and ability to pay." (See chapter 12 on "Alimony" for details.)

How do I begin a court case after my divorce?

If you are unable to work out the after-divorce issue by informal negotiation, mediation, collaborative practice, or negotiation between lawyers, you may ask the court to decide the issue. The legal procedure is to reopen the divorce case. You should file either a petition to change the court order or one for contempt. The court has fill-in-the-blank forms to do this. These forms are available at court or on the state court web site. Use the "change court order" form if you want a change, and the "contempt" form if you want to enforce the order.

If someone is not living up to the court order, he or she may be found in "contempt of court" and ordered to pay the innocent person's attorney's fees. However, attorney's fees are not always awarded. The person filing the petition or motion should expect to pay for his or her own lawyer. If the contempt is serious enough or is repeated, it is within the power of the court to order that the person be arrested and jailed.

The court may order after-divorce cases to mediation. It is most likely to do this if there are significant parenting issues. Parenting coordination is another decision-making option if there are problems with co-parenting. The parenting coordinator works with parents to improve communication, mediate disputes, and if necessary, decide minor practical issues (see page 60).

∞

more
tax tips

appendix
A

More Tax Tips

by Hollis McGuire, MBA, CPA

(Updated by Timothy R. Hepburn, CPA, MBA)

Why are "tax brackets" important to tax planning?

The rate charged for federal income tax depends on your income. At the lowest level, the tax rate is zero, as some income is not taxed. The first rate charged is 10 percent, and the rates increase, currently, to 15 percent, 25 percent, 28 percent and 35 percent. You pay the higher rates only on the amounts in that bracket. Therefore, if you are $1 into a higher bracket, only that $1 is taxed at the higher percentage.

If you and your spouse will be in different tax brackets after your divorce, your decisions on the various tax issues should take into account minimizing taxes for both of you. Discuss your options with a CPA or tax attorney.

How do I choose between standard and itemized deductions?

The tax savings from the standard deduction vary, based on filing status and income.

Costs that qualify for itemization include: medical expenses which exceed certain limits, qualified mortgage interest, property taxes paid, state taxes paid (such as the town or city part of your vehicle registration or any state income tax), and charitable contributions. For many taxpayers, using the standard deduction reduces taxes more than itemized deductions.

For example, if you are in the 28 percent tax bracket and you have a property tax deduction of $4,000, your tax bill would be reduced by $1,120. In this case, if the property tax is the only qualifying expense you have, you would take the standard deduction, as it is larger than this deduction for property tax under all filing statuses.

For some, the deduction may be limited by the Alternative Minimum Tax (AMT). If you are over 65, or if you are blind, additional deductions apply. For these and other deduction issues, get advice from your accountant.

How much is an exemption worth?

Many people believe that an exemption for a child results in major tax savings, but this is not always the case. The 2007 exemption amount is $3,400 for each dependent who is either a "qualifying child" or "qualifying relative" as defined later in this appendix. Therefore, if you are in the 15 percent tax bracket, the savings will be $510, and in the 35 percent tax bracket, the savings could be as high as $1,190 (before any income phase-out consideration).

However, the value of the dependency exemption is usually increased by one or both of the key tax credits that are directly linked to the exemption: (a) the child tax credit; and (b) the education credits. As noted in Chapter 14, the child tax credit provides up to a $1,000 tax credit for each child under age seventeen at the close of the tax year. The child tax credit is calculated using the parent's modified Adjusted Gross Income (AGI) and the credit is reduced when AGI (2007) exceeds $75,000 for single/head of households and $55,000 for married filing separately. (See IRS Publication 972 for the calculation worksheet.) In addition to the child tax credit, the education credits (Hope Scholarship Credit or Lifetime Learning Credit as outlined later in this appendix) benefit only the parent who claims the dependency exemption.

The parent with whom the child lives most of the year, who relinquishes the dependency exemption, may still claim the credit for child and dependent care expenses that he or she alone pays and can also claim the Earned Income Credit,

EIC. See IRS Publication 503 and Form 2441 about child and dependent care expenses and IRS Publication 596 about earned income credit. The table below summarizes the allocation of these tax credits.

Impact on use of four tax credits—claiming the dependency exemption

There are four tax credits that may be claimed for a child. Who may claim each of them depends on which parent the child lives with most of the year. For simplicity, I will call this the "lives with most" parent, and refer to the other parent as the "lives with less" parent. If the "lives with most" parent claims the child as a dependent, he or she may claim all four credits. The chart shows who may claim each tax credit if the "lives with less" parent claims the child dependency exemption.

	"Lives with less" Parent	"Lives with more" Parent
1. Credit for Child and Dependent Care Expenses	No	Yes
2. Earned Income Credit—for *the* Qualifying Child	No	Yes
3. Child Tax Credit	Yes	No
4. Educational Credit(s)	Yes	No

(*The table above considers only one child—potential variations can occur with additional children and each parent having at least one "lives with most" child.*)

The advantage of the higher-income parent claiming the dependency exemption and the two linked credits has some limits. At higher incomes, as indicated above, the amount you (or the other parent) can claim as a deduction or credit is reduced or eliminated. As a result, figuring out which parent would save the most by claiming the dependency exemption each year is a complicated task. It is best to have a CPA or tax preparer do a side by side calculation to see who will benefit not only from the value of the dependency exemption but the two valuable credits that are linked to the dependency exemption—the child tax credit and the educational credits.

Who can qualify as your dependent? Who is a "qualifying child" or "qualifying relative"?

The Internal Revenue Service permits an annual exemption for each person you can claim as a dependent. The term dependent means either a "qualifying child" or a "qualifying relative." There is an initial 3-part test: you are not eligible to be claimed as a dependent, the child or relative is not filing a joint return with spouse, and child or relative is a U.S. citizen or resident alien or resident of Canada or Mexico.

- In most cases, a child of divorced or separated parents will qualify as a dependent of the parent with whom the child lives most of the year. For more specifics on "qualifying relative," see IRS Publication 501.

- To be a "qualifying child" for the purposes of claiming a dependence exemption, a child must be your son, daughter, stepchild, eligible foster child, or a descendant. Three other tests must be met:

  - *Age*—A child must be either under age 19 at the end of the year, a full-time college student under age 24 at the end of the year or permanently or totally disabled at any time of the year, regardless of age.

  - *Residency*—A child lived with you for more than half of the year (excluding temporary absences), or alternatively, the other parent transferred the exemption to you.

  - *Support*—The child must not have provided more than half of his or her own support during the year in question.

Sometimes following divorce, a child is "qualified" with respect to both parents. If the parents cannot agree who will claim the child, the IRS will apply the tie-breaker rule. The tie-breaker rule leans toward providing the qualifying child to the parent whom the child lived with for the longest period of time during the year, and if this is in dispute the qualifying child generally goes to the parent with the highest adjusted gross income (AGI).

What are the specific education tax incentives?

Education tax benefits are available to the parent who claims the annual dependency exemption. The Hope Scholarship Credit applies to tuition and related fees paid to an eligible institution for the first two years of post-secondary education. The student must carry at least a half-time course load. The maximum credit is $1,650 annually per student, covering 100 percent of the first $1,100 of eligible expenses, and 50 percent of the second $1,100. Income limitations apply: for 2007, phase-out ranges are $47,000 to $57,000 for single filers and head of household filers, and $104,000 to $114,000 for joint filers. You cannot claim the Hope Scholarship Credit if your adjusted income exceeds $57,000 (or $114,000 on a joint return).

The Lifetime Learning Credit applies to undergraduate, graduate, and professional degree course work, as well as course work to improve job skills, taken at an eligible educational institution. There is no half-time or greater enrollment requirement. The maximum credit is $2,000 per return filed. This means 20 percent of tuition and fees up to $10,000 a year, regardless of the number of students. The income limitations are the same as for the Hope Scholarship Credit. Currently, there is no limit on the number of years you may claim the Lifetime Learning Credit.

Up to $2,500 of interest paid on qualified loans for higher education is deductible whether you claim the standard deduction or itemize. The student may be you or your child or spouse. Phase-out ranges are $55,000 to $70,000 for single filers and head of household filers, and $110,000 to $140,000 for those married filing a joint tax return.

It is important to note that you may not claim both the Hope Credit and the Lifetime Learning Credit for the same student in a single tax year. You may not claim either credit if the student receives a tax-free distribution from an education IRA. You may, however, claim the Hope Credit for one student and the Lifetime Learning Credit for another, provided the requirements are met.

The Tax Relief and Health Care Act of 2006 has extended the deduction of up to $4,000 for higher education tuition and fees through December 31, 2007.

Can paying house expenses qualify as alimony?

The ownership of the home plays a part in determining which of any payments can be considered alimony and how much can be taken as a deduction. It makes a difference whether:

- the person making the payment has any ownership interest in the house,
- the property is held in joint tenancy or as tenants-in-common, or
- the name of the person in the house is on the mortgage.

Remember, other house-related deductions still apply. The portion of interest and real estate paid that does not qualify as alimony may be a deduction. This is a very technical area. You should consult your CPA or talk to an attorney about the tax consequences before including such provisions in your divorce agreement.

What is alimony recapture?

Alimony recapture is having to list as income on your tax return amounts that you had previously deducted as alimony.

In general, the recapture rules apply if alimony paid in the second or third year decreases by more than $15,000 from the prior year. The decrease could be because payments were not made on time, or there was a change in the divorce agreement, or the court ordered a change because of a reduction in your support needs or in the ability of your former spouse to provide support. Payments made under temporary support orders, fixed-income payments from a business or property, employment compensation and payments that decrease because of the death of either spouse or the remarriage of the spouse receiving the payment are not included in calculations for recapture.

If the recapture rules apply, the alimony payer may have to include in his or her income in the third year part of the alimony payments he or she took as a deduction previously. In turn, the person who received the alimony would be able to take that amount as a deduction in the third year.

What happens to "tax basis" when assets are transferred?

When property is transferred as part of a divorce, the "tax basis" of the property goes with the transfer. The basis is generally the amount originally paid for the property, including fees related to the purchase, such as sales tax, recording fees, or commissions. Example: a husband transfers stock worth $200,000 to his wife. He originally paid $50,000 for the stock plus $5,000 in fees, giving him a basis of $55,000. If the wife then sells the stock for $200,000, she would have to pay tax on a $145,000 gain. It is clear from this example that the basis and the cost of taxes must be considered in any property division.

Is there a tax on income resulting from the property division?

Although property divisions between divorcing spouses are neither reported nor taxed, any income on the assets you receive or produce is reported and taxed. For example, if you receive a bank account with a $10,000 balance, and it earns $500 in interest income, you will be taxed on the $500 interest, but not on the $10,000.

Dividing retirement benefits does not result in any tax obligation. However, if either spouse withdraws funds from a retirement account, he or she will owe taxes and, in many cases, penalties.

One caution with regard to New Hampshire: your change in marital status to single may make you subject to filing a New Hampshire Interest and Dividends Tax return and paying this tax (see below).

New Hampshire tax on interest and dividends

New Hampshire has no personal income tax on wages, pensions, capital gains, and most forms of federally taxable income. In New Hampshire there is a 5 percent personal tax on interest and dividends. This tax applies to taxable interest and dividends totaling more than $2,400 for a single person, $4,800 for a married couple (higher for those over 65 or disabled). The New Hampshire Interest and Dividends Tax has two filing statuses: individual and joint. Divorce will change your filing status and thus may change your need to file this return.

There is no special change of address form for the New Hampshire Department of Revenue. You can either inform the DOR by letter, or wait until you file and use the new address.

What about New Hampshire's taxes on businesses?

New Hampshire imposes a Business Profits Tax and Business Enterprise Tax on businesses. These include businesses formed as sole proprietorships, corporations and partnerships.

There is also a business tax on rental income. Therefore, if the spouse receives the business or rental property as part of the divorce settlement, the state tax consequence should be considered (along with the federal tax consequence) as part of the settlement.

If a spouse owns or becomes the owner of a business operated as a sole proprietorship, he or she must file a Schedule C with each federal income tax return (a Schedule E, page 1, if a landlord with rental property). If the business has gross revenue greater than $50,000 and the federal return contains a Schedule C and/or a Schedule E, page 1, a New Hampshire business return may be required. Time to consult a CPA or tax attorney!

standard order
of paragraphs

appendix
B

Note: Court forms and instructions are available through the Self-Help Center at: www.courts.state.nh.us.

Standard Order of Paragraphs for Final Decree (2005)

Instructions: the paragraph numbers and captions as set forth below shall be used in all final divorce or legal separation decrees. (There is also a standard temporary domestic order of paragraphs that is described below.) You must file an agreed upon or proposed final decree prior to your final hearing, and may use the format below or complete the court's Final Decree on Divorce or Legal Separation form. If a particular paragraph is not needed, it must appear, but may be marked "Not Applicable" or "The parties own no real estate," etc. Consecutive paragraphs may be combined for these purposes, for example, "Paragraphs 12–15: The parties have no business interests, debt or real estate."

1. Type of Case
2. Parenting Plan and Uniform Support Order
3. Tax Exemptions for Children
4. Guardian *ad Litem* Fees
5. Alimony
6. Health Insurance for Spouse
7. Life Insurance
8. Motor Vehicles
9. Furniture and Other Personal Property
10. Retirement Plans and Other Tax-Deferred Assets
11. Other Financial Assets
12. Business Interests of the Parties
13. Division of Debt
14. Marital Home

15. Other Real Property

16. Enforceability after Death

17. Signing of Documents

18. Restraining Order

19. Name Change

20. Other Requests

    Attorney's Fees

    Tax Refunds

    Disclosure of Assets

    Mutual Releases

    Obligations

    Change in Address or Employment

    Miscellaneous

Standard Order of Paragraphs for Temporary Decree

This is the same as the final for numbers 1 to 16; beginning with number 17 there are differences. The temporary numbers are:

17. Restraints against Property

18. Restraining Order

19. Other Requests

(There is no number 20.)

Parenting Plan

Standard order of paragraphs: All parties in cases seeking parental rights and responsibilities for minor children must file an agreed upon or proposed Parenting Plan prior to the temporary hearing and the final hearing. You may complete the court's Parenting Plan form, or may create your own document. If you choose to create your own document, you must follow the standard order of lettered paragraphs set forth below.

State whether it is a temporary or final plan, or a change to an earlier plan. Print the names and dates of birth for each child involved in the parenting plan.

A. *Decision-Making Responsibility*
    Major Decisions
    Day-to Day Decisions
    Other

B. *Residential Responsibility & Parenting Schedule*
    Routine Schedule
    Holiday and Birthday Planning
    Three-day Weekends
    Vacation Schedule
    Supervised Parenting Time
    Other Parental Responsibilities

C. *Legal Residence of a Child for School Attendance*

D. *Transportation & Exchange of the Child(ren)*

E. *Information Sharing & Access, Including Telephone & Electronic Access*
    Parent-Child Telephone Contact
    Parent-Child Written Communication

F. *Relocation of a Residence of a Child*

G. *Procedure for Review & Adjustment of Parenting Plan*

H. *Method(s) for Resolving Disputes*

I. *Other Parenting Agreements*

∞

How to Understand the Standard Order of Paragraphs

The New Hampshire Family Division has lists of Standard Paragraphs for temporary and permanent agreements (decrees) and for parenting plans. These require that the various issues be dealt with in a specific order. The following material was written by the author to help you understand these Standard Paragraphs and the issues involved in any divorce agreement and parenting plan. (See the previous section of this appendix for the official Standard Order of Paragraphs.)

All agreements submitted to the court, whether worked out informally by the divorcing couple, mediated and drafted by neutrals, or negotiated in collaborative practice or through lawyers and drafted by lawyers, must follow the **standard numbering and lettering.** They must also be used in proposed orders submitted to the court for contested hearings. If any issue does not apply to you, it can be filled in "not applicable."

Final and Temporary Agreements

By reviewing the 20 standard paragraphs for final decrees and those for parenting plans (if you have minor children), you will better understand the many topics that must be covered in your divorce. The standard paragraphs for a temporary decree are the same, except for paragraphs 17–20. For a further explanation of the topics, review the appropriate chapter. For the meaning of any technical terms, check the index and the definitions section at the back of this book.

The 20 Standard Paragraphs for Final Decree:

1. Type of Case: This must include a statement that there will be a divorce, and the grounds for it.

While any divorce results in both spouses being divorced, paragraph one must state who "is granted" the divorce. The divorce may be granted to the husband, wife, or both. (The legal effect is identical: both are divorced. The choice is usually based on psychological or other personal reasons.)

If the parties filed a joint petition, then either "we" or "the parties" are listed as receiving. If only one spouse requested the divorce, he or she is usually the recipient. However, by agreement, the divorce may be awarded to both. If only husband or wife receives the divorce, he or she must be the person filing for the divorce.

Virtually all agreed-on divorces are based on "irreconcilable differences, which have caused the irremediable breakdown of the marriage." (If a contested divorce is requested based on fault, the proposed order will say so here.)

2. Parenting Plan and Uniform Support Order: If you have minor children, this paragraph will say that a parenting plan and a uniform support order (USO) are attached. The USO is a form required in every case with a minor child or child support. Technically, this paragraph may say simply "See attached parenting plan and USO." Many couples also wish to state the amount of child support and frequency in paragraph 2. For example, "Jean shall pay Jody child support of $150 each week. See USO for specifics." If there are no minor children, this paragraph will state "not applicable."

3. Tax Exemptions for Children: Who will get the exemptions, or will they be divided? Will it be the same for all future years, alternate (odd/even) or some other plan? Will receipt of exemption be tied to being current in support for the tax year? The court's fill-in-the-blank form includes only some of the choices. For instance, if there are three children, each could get one exemption and the third exemption could be split. Review chapter 14 on taxes for information.

4. GAL Fees/Court Fund Reimbursement: If there is a guardian *ad litem*, the final allocation of fees is spelled out here.

5. Alimony: If there is to be spousal support, the amount and frequency of payment must be stated. Are payments to change over time? What factors (such as living with an unrelated adult or remarriage) would cause alimony to either be reviewed or to end? For federal tax purposes, the agreement should state that alimony ends if the recipient dies.

6. Health Insurance for Spouse: Will one spouse or spouse's employer continue to cover the other for some period? If there is an additional premium for the former spouse, who will pay? Will either spouse pay some or all of the other's uninsured costs? If each has his/her own insurance, this paragraph may say: "Each shall provide his/her own health insurance and pay his/her own uninsured costs."

7. Life Insurance: The purpose of this section is to protect against the ending of child support, alimony, or other payments due to the death of the paying person. It may also insure payment of a joint debt. The paragraph should specify who is to be insured, the amount of death benefit, the period for which insurance is required, the beneficiary (and, if the beneficiary is a minor, the trustee), and the frequency for documenting that the insurance is in place.

If there is cash-value life insurance (whole life), ownership of the policy may be awarded in this paragraph or with other financial assets in paragraph 15.

8. Motor Vehicles: Be specific as to who gets which vehicle. Usually the brand and year is sufficient. If there are vehicles of the same brand and year, add model or color. Note that the category is "vehicles"—include trucks, off-road vehicles, snowmobiles, boats, etc. If monthly payments or any other expenses will be paid by the other person, note it in this paragraph. One or more of the vehicles may be either in joint names or in the name of the person who is not receiving it. The agreement should provide for transfer of title, as needed.

9. Furniture and Other Personal Property: If the parties have separated, it may be possible to state that each gets what he or she currently has possession of; or the person who moved out may be getting a few items, in addition to what he or she already has. However, if the parties have not yet separated, a more detailed list is needed.

Two commonly used methods involve listing items and attaching the list to the agreement: a single list of all house contents, with the first name or the initials of the spouse getting the item; or a separate list for each spouse, labeled " Paragraph 9 —What Husband Gets" and " Paragraph 9—What Wife Gets."

10. Retirement Plans and Other Tax-Deferred Assets: If each spouse is getting to keep his or her retirement plans, it can be said simply: " Husband shall receive his Conway pension, his Keene 401(k), and his Pelham IRA. Wife shall receive her Portsmouth pension."

Usually retirement plans are divided between the spouses, and several specifics are required: date of division, how much the non-employee spouse gets, and who will draft the QDRO. The agreement should outline all the substantive terms for the QDRO. It can be useful to include a deadline for getting the QDRO drafted. If any retirement plan is being divided, please note it usually takes months to accomplish the division.

If a defined contribution plan is to be split 50/50, say, "wife will receive 50% of husband's Sunapee 401(k) as of the date of the division." If the non-employee is to get a specific amount, the parties may want to specify the date the dollar amount was calculated and provide that the amount be adjusted for losses and gains from that date to the distribution.

Defined benefit plans require the most specifics:

    a. Percentage to non-employee

    b. Time period used in calculation (Hodgins or other)

    c. Single annuity with survivor annuity or separate annuity

See chapter 13 for more about dividing retirement plans. Warning: This is a very technical area requiring legal advice.

11. Other Financial Assets: If there are no joint accounts or other joint financial assets and each is to keep his/her own, simply say it. If there are joint financial assets, each asset must be allocated to one spouse or divided. The best practice is to include specifics: financial institution, type of account or investment, number of shares or bonds. If the split of an asset is 50/50, it will usually be as of the date of split. However, if one spouse is to get a specific amount from the other's account, delays in the split could be unfair. A time frame for carrying out the division, such as "within 30 days," could be helpful.

12. Business Interests: In some cases, the business may be a part-time sideline. Frequently, such entities are going to the spouse who operates: "Wife shall receive all rights to her Mary Kay business." If the spouse is being bought out, specify the payments, the timing of them, and any security for them. If the business is more than a sideline, advice from a CPA or lawyer is needed on valuation, tax factors, timing of buyout, and stock transfers.

13. Division of Debt: Debt may be viewed as a negative asset. Joint debts can be problematic, as the person who is to pay may fail to do so. If there are liquid assets, using some of them to pay off (or down) joint debts will benefit the parties' future relationship. If it is the time of year when a tax refund is anticipated, the refund (paragraph 20) may be applied to one or more specific debts.

List charge cards specifically, including bank name. Most people intend that joint accounts no longer be used. If this is agreed, say so. It is important to include a "hold harmless" clause such as: "Each spouse will hold harmless the other as to all debts he or she is to pay." This may provide some protection to the person whose former spouse fails to pay as agreed.

14. Marital Home: Will one spouse get the house or will it be sold? Sometimes, one spouse gets the use of the home for a time period (such as one year, five years, or until age eighteen of a child), after which it is sold and the net proceeds divided. If the house is sold, what formula will be used to divide the proceeds; 50/50, 60/40, or a set amount to one spouse, balance to the other?

How will mortgage, taxes, insurance, maintenance, and repairs be handled? In some delayed sales, one spouse fronts the money for repairs, but is repaid from the proceeds before the property split.

If the sale is delayed even for a few months, there is the important issue of the form of ownership. Will it be kept as joint tenants with rights of survivorship or change to tenants-in-common? If one spouse should die before the sale, this choice would produce substantially different results. Under a right of survivorship, the other spouse will be the sole owner; with tenants-in-common, the survivor and the other's estate will be co-owners.

If one person is getting all the equity in the house, what about the mortgage? Will it be refinanced now or within a set period; or is the other person willing to have his or her ability to borrow and credit rating tied to a joint mortgage for many years?

If you own a home, get legal advice on this part of the agreement.

15. Other Real Property: This paragraph includes any other real estate, such as vacation homes, time-shares, rental property, and commercial property. Similar considerations apply as those for paragraph 14, although "other real estate" is more often sold at divorce. If this has been depreciated (example: rental property), there may be tax consequences.

16. Enforceability after Death: If either spouse dies before all the provisions of the agreement are carried out, will his or her estate have the obligation to carry out the agreement? For instance, if the estate is to make payments (such as alimony or child support) required under the agreement: "The terms of this agreement shall be a charge against the estate of each." If life insurance is to cover certain expenses, add a phrase such as "except that if the life insurance required under paragraph 7 exists, the obligation of child support shall not be a charge."

17. Signing of Documents: This paragraph specifies a time period, typically thirty or sixty days for the preparation and signing of documents needed to carry out the agreement. These documents may include deeds, mortgages, vehicle titles, IRS forms, and QDROs.

18. Restraining Order: If either party is restricted from harassment, or entering the other's home or work place, it must be stated here. Often, restraining orders apply to both parties.

19. Name Change: If either spouse is resuming a former name, it should be specified here. For example, "wife shall resume her maiden name of Janet Boudreau."

20. Other Requests:

    A. Attorney's Fees: There are two parts to this: The attorney's fees for the divorce and possible future attorney's fees if either person fails to live up to the terms of the agreement. Will each person pay his or her own divorce fees, will they be paid from joint funds, or will one spouse pay both lawyers? (Unless neither spouse has a lawyer, this information should be included.)

    B. Tax Refunds: If the couple is going to file jointly, state it here and specify how any deficit will be paid and any refund allocated. Some couples agree to apply the refund to a joint debt.

    C. Disclosure of Assets: This is a statement that each has honestly listed all known assets on his/her financial affidavit.

    D. Mutual Releases: Each releases the other from

any obligations, except those specified in the decree, USO, or other court order.

E. Obligations: Except as provided in the decree, each is responsible for any debt he/she has incurred.

F. Change in address or employment: If there are ongoing responsibilities such as child support, alimony, insurance, or delayed division of an asset, each should be required to keep the other informed on his/her address. If there is a "material change" in employment such as availability of insurance or substantial income change, the other person must be notified.

G. Miscellaneous: This is the place to include any provision that did not fit elsewhere in the decree.

Parenting Plans

Every parenting plan should give the name(s) and birth date of the child or children it applies to. It should state whether it is a temporary plan, final plan, or one changing a prior plan or order. The court's fill-in-the-blank form has sections on page one to fill in this information.

The standard paragraphs of the parenting plan:

A. Decision-Making Responsibility

Major Decisions—New Hampshire has a presumption of joint decision-making and access to information. Will these be decided jointly or by one parent?

Day-to Day Decisions

Other—Many agreements provide some specifics, such as listing or describing the sort of decisions to be jointly made. Some specify how decisions for the child will be made if the parents disagree

B. Residential Responsibility & Parenting Schedule

This section describes the parenting schedule. Many parents just describe the schedule, and avoid giving either parent the title of "primary." Most families do best with specifics on the weekly schedule, school vacations, holidays, and children's birthdays. The purposes of the specifics include:

- Predictable time with each parent, allowing parents and children to plan their lives.

- Although it can be adjusted by agreement, the printed schedule operates as a default schedule, if agreement is not possible.

Routine Schedule—What will be the schedule for each one or two week period? Be specific as to both days and times. For instance: We shall share the parenting of the children on a 2-2-3 day schedule exchanging the children at 6 p.m. Sunday, 6 p.m. Tuesday, and 6 p.m. Thursday.

Holiday and Birthday Planning—Most parents include a schedule for holidays important to their family. Be specific as to any alternation between parents and beginning and ending times. For instance: We shall share Thanksgiving with one parent having from Wednesday after school to 5 p.m. Thursday and the other parent having from 5 p.m. Thursday to 5 p.m. Friday. Terry shall have the first period in even-numbered years and Kerry shall have the first period in odd-numbered years.

Three-day Weekends—If you are alternating weekends, you may want Monday holidays to go with the weekend. Over time, each of you will get some 3-day weekends; or your family may want a more detailed plan.

Vacation Schedule—Will either of you have the child for a school vacation week, or any time during the summer? Some parents alternate the school vacation weeks (mother in odd-numbered years, father in even-numbered years), others use the same schedule every year. For summer vacations, it can be helpful to include a notice requirement: Each may have the children for up to 2 weeks in the summer, provided that notice is given by May 1.

Supervised Parenting Time—Use this section if either parent's time with the child must be in the presence of a specified person or at a "visitation center." In all other cases, state "not applicable."

Other Parental Responsibilities—This is used to fill in details to fit each family. Common provisions are promoting a good relationship with the other parent, seeing that the children get to extra-curricular activities, and not abusing alcohol when the children are present.

C. Legal Residence of a Child for School Attendance

School districts do not want to be caught in the middle. If a child lives in one district most of the time, that is where the child will go to school. If the child spends approximately equal time with parents in different school districts, you must specify which will be the legal residence for school purpose.

D. Transportation & Exchange of the Child(ren)

How will the child get between one parent's house and the other? Will one parent do all the transportation? If it will be shared, be specific about what part each parent will do. If there is a substantial distance between homes, there may be plane fares or other costs. How will they be paid?

E. Information Sharing & Access, Including Telephone & Electronic Access

It is important to keep the other parent informed of any emergency or significant decisions about the child. Most parents agree to send the other parent copies of school reports and information on school events.

Parent-Child Telephone Contact—Some specify when the parent not having care of the child may phone.

Parent-Child Written Communication—Will there by any specifics for e-mail or other written communication?

F. Relocation of a Residence of a Child

New Hampshire law spells out the procedure, and legal test if a parent the child lives with for 150 days a year wishes to move. Some parents agree to modify this procedure, work out a different procedure and text or agree to limit how far either will move: "We agree to continue to live within 20 miles of Milford Town Hall."

G. Procedure for Review & Adjustment of Parenting Plan

Unless your only child is 16 or 17 years old, likely you will need to make changes in the parenting plan. The best approach is to agree to review the plan for possible changes at specified times once or twice a year.

H. Method(s) for Resolving Disputes

If you used mediation or collaborative practice to work out your parenting plan, you may wish to say that you would use that procedure in the future, before litigation.

I. Other Parenting Agreements

Use this for any provision that did not fit in sections A to H.

checklists
and
resources

appendix

C

Things to Do
After Your Divorce

This list includes steps commonly needed after a divorce. Not all of them will apply to you. Some will require the assistance of your lawyer.

☐ Adjust your dealings with the other parent to a child-centered and "businesslike" approach.

☐ Notify child's school, pediatrician, and dentist about decision-making responsibility, addresses, phone numbers.

☐ Arrange to pick up personal property or have the other person do so.

☐ Send change of address forms (available at your post office) to the US Postal Service, insurance companies, banks, investment companies, healthcare providers, Department of Motor Vehicles.

☐ Sign over vehicle title, or get other side to sign over vehicle title.

☐ Be sure vehicle insurance is in your name and at your current address.

☐ Remove the other side's name from bank accounts, bonds, charge cards, and other financial arrangements.

☐ Pay money owed — or set up wage assignment.

☐ Change the amount and beneficiaries of your life insurance.

☐ Arrange for after-divorce health insurance for yourself or your former spouse.

❑ If you are changing your name, take the necessary steps with your employer, bank, Social Security Administration, and Department of Motor Vehicles.

❑ Prepare a QDRO and get it approved by Plan Administrator (lawyer required).

❑ Update your will (lawyer required).

❑ Sign and record any deeds or mortgages.

❑ Change homeowner insurance to match any change in ownership.

❑ Send in IRS Form 8822 with change of address and status (also see tax checklist in chapter 14).

❑ Mark your calendar for future steps required under your divorce agreement or orders:

   ❑ Review child support in three years (or sooner if your divorce papers say so).

   ❑ Provide or request IRS Form 8332 to transfer exemption for child.

   ❑ Document that you have the required life insurance or request such documentation from the other parent.

   ❑ Account to the other parent for child's funds.

❑ Let go of the past and focus on the future.

∝∞

Resources for Divorce

This is only a partial listing and is subject to change. Consult the community or yellow pages of your local phone directory for other organizations and professionals. Support groups are sometimes organized by local churches/synagogues and by mental health organizations and private psychotherapists. Check in your area.

New Hampshire Services and Information (except as noted, area code is 603)

Domestic Violence—New Hampshire Help Line
1-800-852-3388 (in-state only); 225-9000.

Provides referrals to local hotlines and support groups.

Baker Newman & Noyes, LLC
1-800-244-7444
650 Elm Street, Suite 302
Manchester, NH   03101
www.bnnopn.com
e-mail: thepburn@bnncpa.com

Certified Public Accountants. Offer tax advice and preparation. Additional services for those facing divorce include financial planning and advice during mediation, collaborative practice, negotiation, and litigation.

Catholic Charities—Office of Family Ministries.
669-3030; 1-800-562-5249 (in-state only)
www.catholiccharities.org

Information on many topics including: support groups, parenting info. Brochure available on church annulment. Has current listings for local support groups, including: Separated and Divorced Catholics, and Rainbows (for children who have suffered a loss through death or divorce).

Fair Solutions
654-5000
Mediation Location: 17 Main Street, Wilton
Mailing Address: P.O. Box 1112, Wilton, NH 03086
www.nhdivorce.com

Honey Hastings, JD, uses mediation and parenting coordination to assist divorcing couples in making the decisions for their families. She also assists with other family issues, including premarital agreements, unwed disputes, grandparents' rights, and family businesses.

Family Resource Connection
1-800-298-4321 (toll free)
www.state.nh.us/nhsl/frc

Service of the New Hampshire State Library. Source of information on various topics including parenting, divorce, step-parenting, etc. Has a lending library of books. Maintains an online calendar of events (state-wide) for citizens and professionals on family topics.

Honey Hastings, JD
654-5000
P. O. Box 1112
Wilton, NH 03086
www.nhdivorce.com

Legal services regarding New Hampshire family law, including: consultations, second opinions, advice during mediation, Collaborative Practice, negotiation of disputed issues, unbundled legal services. Her web site has information on New Hampshire divorce procedure and law, and services available.

Info Link
1-888-499-2525 (toll free)
www.infolinknh.org

Offers information for seacoast area on various topics and services, including divorce, parenting and support groups.

Legal Advice and Referral Center (LARC)
1-800-639-5290 or 224-3333

PO Box 4147
Concord, NH 03301-4147
www.larcnh.org

Contact LARC if you need legal advice and cannot afford a lawyer. LARC provides free information, legal advice, and referral services to low-income persons concerning family law, local welfare, and housing. Qualified individuals needing legal representation are referred to the NH Bar Association's Pro Bono Referral Program. LARC also has pamphlets on Divorce/ Separation, Parenting Rights, Child Support, and Domestic Violence.

New Hampshire Bar Association
224-6942
2 Pillsbury Street, Suite 300
Concord, NH 03301
www.nhbar.org

All lawyers in New Hampshire are members of the New Hampshire Bar Association. The Bar Association offers pamphlets on Divorce and other family law topics. These pamphlets are available from the NH Bar, by mail or on their web site (see address above). Other Bar Association services for the public may be found at http://nhbar.org/for-the-public/free-legal-services.asp:

- *Lawyer Referral Service*: **229-0002**
  LRS provides referrals statewide for those who can afford to pay for an attorney's services. The service will provide the name of a lawyer in your area who handles cases of the type you have.
  For e-mail referrals: **lrsreferral@nhbar.org**

- *Reduced Fee Referral Program*: **229-0002**
  Reduced Fee provides referrals statewide to qualified individuals who can afford to pay something for legal services, but who cannot afford a lawyer's regular fees.

- *The Pro Bono Program*: (Call Legal Advice and Referral Center at **1-800-639-5290 or 224-3333**)
  Pro Bono links low-income people in need of legal

260 260 Hastings / THE NEW HAMPSHIRE DIVORCE HANDBOOK

representation with volunteer lawyers who provide services at no charge, in the areas of family law, bankruptcy, landlord-tenant issues, and children's disability. Individuals are qualified for Pro Bono assistance through the Legal Advice and Referral Center at the phone numbers or address listed above.

- *LawLine*: **1-800-868-1212**
  A monthly call-in service of the Bar Association, staffed by volunteer lawyers. LawLine provides free legal information on the second Wednesday of each month from 6 p.m. to 8 p.m.

- *The DOVE Project*
  The DOVE Project provides free legal representation at final restraining order hearings for qualifying survivors of domestic violence. For referral to Project, contact New Hampshire Coalition Against Domestic & Sexual Violence listed on page 261.

New Hampshire Board of Guardian ad Litem *Certification*
271-1199
State House Annex
25 Capitol Street, Room 120
Concord, NH 03301
www.nh.gov/gal/certified.htm

The board certifies guardians *ad litem* who meet the legal requirements. A list of Certified Guardians *ad Litem* is available from the board.

New Hampshire Board of Marital Mediation Certification
271-6593
State House Annex, Room 424
25 Capitol Street
Concord, NH 03301
www.nh.gov/marital

The board certifies mediators who meet the legal requirements. A list of Certified Marital Mediators is available from the board.

New Hampshire Child Care Resource & Referral Network
www.nhccrr.org

Lists sources of child care and other services for parents, by town or city.

New Hampshire Coalition Against Domestic & Sexual Violence
1-866-644-3574 (for domestic violence)
1-800-277-5570 (for sexual violence)
4 South State Street
Concord, NH 03301
www.nhcadsv.org

Information on domestic violence and referrals to local groups.
Offers a free brochure on stalking.

New Hampshire Commission on the Status of Women
271-2660
State House Annex, Room 414
25 Capitol Street
Concord, NH 03301
www.nh.gov/csw

Offers booklet entitled, *A Legal Handbook for Women in New
Hampshire.*

New Hampshire Conflict Resolution Association
230-9903
P.O. Box 3203
Nashua, NH 03061
www.nhcra.org

A voluntary organization of mediators and other conflict
resolution professionals.

New Hampshire Legal Assistance
Claremont: 1-800-562-3994 or 542-8795
Littleton: 1-800-548-1886 or 444-8000
Manchester: 1-800-562-3174 or 668-2900
Nashua: 1-800-517-0577 or 598-3800
Portsmouth: 1-800-334-3135 or 431-7411
http://www.nhla.org/

NHLA provides free legal advice and representation to
low-income people in civil matters involving basic needs
and domestic violence.

New Hampshire, State of
Family Division (court procedures, locations, phones):
http://www.courts.state.nh.us/fdpp/fdpp/index.htm
Legislature (laws and pending legislation):
http://www.gencourt.state.nh.us/ie/
Supreme Court:
www.courts.state.nh.us/supreme/index.htm
Self-help Center:
http://www.courts.state.nh.us

Parents Without Partners—Central New England
669-4275
P. O. Box 4591
Manchester, NH 03108
www.pwp1239.org

Support organization for those who are parenting children alone. Plans discussions and activities for children and adults. (See listing under National Organizations for more information.)

Supervised Visitation Network
www.svnetwork.net/ServiceProviders.html

Lists New Hampshire Visitation Centers, with contact information. Some offer a location to exchange your child; some offer supervised visitation or transportation. Contact the individual organization for more information. Additional centers are being considered in other locations. Call your local court or domestic violence group.

National Organizations

These organizations or agencies have members in New Hampshire, or provide information on divorce and parenting.

American Academy of Matrimonial Lawyers
312-263-6477
150 N. Michigan Avenue, Suite 2040 / Chicago, IL 60601
www.aaml.org

For assistance in locating a family lawyer in your area. Web site includes articles on parenting plans and after-divorce issues. Also publishes books for lay people and professionals about family law.

American Association of Retired Persons
1-888-687-2277
601 E Street, NW / Washington, DC 20049
www.aarp.org

This organization offers a wide range of information for people over fifty. Grandparents Center (ext. 2108) provides brochures and support for grandparents raising children. Also information and publications about pensions. Web site has links to other sites.

American Bar Association
1-800-285-2221
321 N. Clark Street / Chicago, IL 60610
www.abanet.org

National organization for the legal profession. Has information about how to find a lawyer and what to do if you are having problems. Pamphlets and publications available.

Association for Conflict Resolution
202-464-9700
1015 18th Street, NW, Suite 1150
Washington, DC 20036
www.acrnet.org

For assistance in locating a mediator in your area. Web site has good links to family resources and a bookstore with mediation and divorce-related books.

Association of Family and Conciliation Courts
608-664-3750
6525 Grand Teton Plaza / Madison, WI 53719
www.afccnet.org

Publishes videos, books, and ten brochures to assist families facing divorce. Information on parenting coordination, including the Model Standards. To the public they offer referral services for lawyers, mediators, and social workers in your area.

Children's Rights Council
301-559-3120
6200 Editors Park Drive, Suite 103 / Hyattsville, MD 20782
www.crckids.org

Has information on parenting issues and divorce reform; books on children's issues.

Internal Revenue Service
1-800-829-3676
www.irs.gov/index.html

Forms are available on the web site. You can get both forms and publications by phoning. Publication 504 is for divorced and separated individuals.

National Center for Missing and Exploited Children
1-800-843-5678
www.missingkids.com

Has a publication called Family Abduction, on preventing and solving abductions.

Office of Child Support Enforcement
202-401-9373
U.S. Department of Health and Human Services
Aerospace Building / 370 L'Enfant Promenade, SW
Washington, DC 20447
www.acf.hhs.gov/programs/cse/

This organization is a Federal/state/local partnership to collect child support. The web site has information about each of the states with their specific requirements for child support.

Older Women's League
1-800-825-3695
3300 N. Fairfax Drive, Suite 218 / Arlington, VA 22201
www.owl-national.org/index.htm

Book available: *Divorce and the Older Woman*

Parents Without Partners
1-800-637-7974
1650 South Dixie Highway, Suite 510 / Boca Raton, FL 33432
www.parentswithoutpartners.org

Support group for single parents. National organization publishes magazine; local groups have informational meetings and social activities.

Pension Appraisal Services
Pension Appraisers
1-800-447-0084
www.pensionappraisers.com

Legal Economic Evaluations, Inc.
1-800-221-6826
www.legaleconomic.com

Office of Children's Issues
1-888-407-4747
Department of State—Office of Children's Issues
SA-29, 2201 C Street, NW
U.S. Department of State
Washington, DC 20520
http://travel.state.gov/family/about/about_605.html

Assists in preventing and solving international abductions.

WISER: Women's Institute for a Secure Retirement
202-393-5452
1725 K St. NW / Washington, DC 20006
www.wiser.heinz.org

This is an independent nonprofit organization devoted to educating women about retirement issues.

Books for Adults and Children

Books marked with a star are especially recommended. Your library or bookstore will either have these books or can order them for you. They can also suggest other helpful books.

For Adults

Be a Great Divorced Dad, Kenneth N. Condrell. (St. Martin's Griffin, 1998. ISBN 0-312-15549-2.) While addressed to fathers, this book offers important insights for mothers as well. Every chapter has practical tips for after-divorce parenting, including dealing with homework, illness, and holidays.

Collaborative Divorce: The Revolutionary New Way to Restructure Your Family, Resolve Legal Issues, and Move on with Your Life, Pauline H. Tesler, Peggy Thompson. (Regan Books, 2006. ISBN 0-06-088943-8.) A guide to the "team model" form of collaborative practice.

★*The Collaborative Way to Divorce: The Revolutionary Method that Results in Less Stress, Lower Costs, and Happier Kids--Without Going to Court*, Ron Ousky, Stuart Webb. (Hudson Street Press, 2006. ISBN 1-59463-022-4.) Explains the difference between traditional and collaborative divorce and gives a step-by-step guide to the collaborative process.

★*Crazy Time: Surviving Divorce and Building a New Life*, Abigail Trafford. (Harper Perennial, 1993. ISBN 0-060-92309-1.) Charts the emotional journey through divorce. Information on coping with loss and failure and dealing with the uncertainty of the future.

Divorce & Money: How to Make the Best Financial Decisions During Divorce, Violet Woodhouse, Victoria Felton-Collins, Ribi Leonard and M. C. Blakeman. (Nolo Press, 1996.

ISBN 0-873-37342-1.) Comprehensive, readable guide to navigate the financial maze of gathering information, generating and assessing options, and reaching financial agreements.

Divorce Without Court: A Guide to Mediation & Collaborative Divorce, Katherine E. Stoner. (Nolo Press, 2006. ISBN 1-4133-0494-X.) Explains the way to get divorced using interest-based negotiation without litigation.

The Divorce Handbook, James T. Friedman. (Random House, 1984. ISBN 0-394-72327-9.) Answers many basic questions, including ones about the litigation process. The suggestions about how to be a better witness are excellent.

The Divorce Mediation Handbook: Everything You Need to Know, Paula James. (Jossey-Bass Publishing [www.josseybass. com], 1997. ISBN 0-787-90872-X.) Helps you answer the question of whether mediation is appropriate for you. Explains the mediation process with tips to help it work.

The Dollars and Sense of Divorce, Judith Briles, Edwin C. Schilling, Carol Ann Wilson. (Dearborn Financial Publishing, 1998. ISBN 0-793-12763-7.) Very readable book that explains the importance of the various financial decisions in a divorce. Many practical tips such as "13 Mistakes Even Smart People Make" and "13 Things Never to Say to Your Soon to Be Ex."

The Good Divorce, Constance Ahrons. (Harper Perennial [www. harpercollins.com], 1994. ISBN 0-060-92634-1.) Shows how couples can move beyond the confusing and frightening early stages of breakup to learn to deal with the transition to a "binuclear" family, a family in two households.

Mom's House, Dad's House: Making Two Homes for Your Child, Isolina Ricci. (Fireside, 1997. ISBN 0-684-83078-7.) Details the principles of two-home parenting and how to set up a shared parenting arrangement that works. Explains the value of having a business-like relationship with the other parent.

New Hampshire Civil Unions Guide (http://nh.glad.org/marriage/ New_Hampshire_Civil_Unions.pdf) Basic information.

★Planning for Shared Parenting: A Guide for Parents Living Apart (www.mass.gov/courts/courtsandjudges/courts/ probateandfamilycourt/afccsharedparenting.pdf.) Discusses children's developmental needs by age groups and how to make a parenting plan, by age of child.

What About the Kids?: Raising Your Children Before, During, and After Divorce, Judith S. Wallerstein, Sandra Blakeslee. (Hyperion [www.hyperionbooks.com], 2003. ISBN 0-7868-6865-1.) Practical advice on children to guide you through divorce and after. Provides help in answering questions children ask.

For Children

Dear Mr. Henshaw, Beverly Cleary. (Avon, 1996. ISBN 0-380-72798-6.) Fiction. In this book ten-year-old Leigh carries on a correspondence with his favorite author. His letters reveal his concerns about growing up and experiencing divorce. A Newbury Medal winner.

★Dinosaurs Divorce, Marc Tolon Brown, and Laurence Krasny Brown. (Little Brown & Co., 1988. ISBN 0-316-11248-8, 0-606-03969-4.) The impact on young dinosaur siblings when their parents divorce. (Preschool to young elementary.)

Family Advocate "My Parents Are Getting Divorced: A Handbook by and for Kids" American Bar Association Family Law Section (Volume 29, No. 1.) This magazine issue has a great deal of information to help young people understand the divorce process, including how to keep track of where you'll be and when. Order from the American Bar Association at 1-800-285-2221. (See additional information under Resources.)

★Mom's House, Dad's House for Kids: Feeling at Home in One Home or Two, Isolina Ricci. (Fireside, 2006. ISBN 0743277120.) The children's version of Dr. Ricci's book on making a shared parenting arrangement work.

∞

definitions

definitions

ADR. Alternate dispute resolution.

adultery. Sexual intercourse between a married person and a person of the opposite sex who is not his/her spouse.

affidavit. A written statement signed and confirmed under oath or affirmation by the party signing it.

alimony. Payments made to or on behalf of a spouse or former spouse under court order.

alternate dispute resolution (ADR). Ways of making decisions and resolving disputes, other than litigation (contested hearings); includes collaborative practice, mediation, parenting coordination, arbitration, and neutral evaluation.

answer. To reply to a petition. Also, the court paper containing the reply. An answer is filed by the respondent.

appeal. To take an unfavorable decision to a higher court in order to request that it be changed. In New Hampshire, appeals of divorce cases go to the New Hampshire Supreme Court.

appear. To file an appearance form, due by the date shown on the order of notice. This is a technical term, and does not mean going to the courthouse. The form may be mailed in.

appearance. A court form that you file to show that you are going to represent yourself, or one that your lawyer files to show that he or she represents you.

appointment order. Court order naming a mediator, guardian *ad litem*, or parenting coordinator. The order is a court form. The judge or master fills in the specifics.

appraisal. Determination of the current value of an asset by a qualified person. Also known as a *valuation*.

arrearage. Amount of child support or alimony that is owed for prior periods.

automatic restraining order. When a divorce is filed, this order takes effect. It restricts both spouses' handling and use of assets.

bailiff. A member of sheriff's staff who maintains security and good order at a courthouse.

case manager. A court staff person who provides information about the law and the court process.

case management conference. A meeting with the case manager about the court process.

chambers' conference. A meeting of the lawyers with the judge or master in his or her office.

child impact program. A required seminar to help parents understand how their children are affected by divorce and how to minimize harm to them during the process.

civil union. A formal legal relationship between two men or two women which in New Hampshire entitles the parties to the same obligations and responsibilities as in a marriage.

clerk. Chief administrator of the Family Division courts in a region of the state. The clerk is assisted by deputy clerks and various support staff.

clerk's office. The administrative office of each court. The clerk's office accepts court papers being filed with the court and issues court orders. Except at hearings, all communication with the court is through the clerk's office.

COBRA. Federal law concerning health insurance coverage after divorce.

collaborative practice (also collaborative law). An ADR method to resolve disputes respectfully. It utilizes specially-trained lawyers, and sometimes other professionals, to help the parties negotiate a mutually acceptable settlement without using the court to decide any issues.

conference. A court event concerning the procedures in a case. Generally, the lawyers must attend. For some conferences the parties must attend; for others, their attendance is optional.

contested divorce. A divorce in which one or more issues are in dispute and must be decided by court.

co-parenting. Both parents actively participate in the child's care and upbringing.

co-respondent. A person whom one spouse names in court papers as having committed adultery with the other spouse.

court. The institution for reviewing, approving, and enforcing agreements, and for resolving disputes, if no agreement is possible. Often used to refer to the judge or master handling a particular case, as in the phrase, "The court denied the motion."

court paper. A document filed at court. Court papers include petitions, motions, objections, and mandatory court forms such as financial affidavits, child support worksheets, and uniform support orders.

court calendar. The schedule of upcoming hearings and conferences in a specific court.

courthouse. The building where the court is; the place where hearings and conferences occur.

courtroom. The room where hearings and conferences occur. It has a formal arrangement of places for judge/master, lawyers, clients, witnesses, and observers.

coverture fraction. Formula for dividing a pension a

spouse receives; half of the benefit, multiplied by the length of the marriage, divided by the total months of employment.

cross-examination. At a hearing or deposition, questions asked of a witness by a lawyer other than the lawyer who called the witness.

cross-petition. A respondent's court papers that request a divorce or other action by the court.

custody. Rights concerning a child. This term is no longer used in New Hampshire divorce, after divorce, or unwed family cases.

decision-making responsibility. The responsibility to make major decisions for your child.

decree. A written court order or decision.

default. The respondent fails to respond to court papers by filing an appearance. Also, the court may find a default against any party failing to attend a hearing, answer interrogatories, or obey court rules. (In a default, the court order is made without information from the defaulted party.)

defendant. The former term for a person who receives court papers from his/her spouse, other parent, or another family member. This person is now called the *respondent*.

deposition. A type of discovery, usually held in a lawyer's office. One party to the case is questioned under oath by the other party's lawyer. A court reporter is present and records the questions and answers.

direct examination. At a hearing or deposition, questions asked of a witness by the lawyer who called the witness.

discovery. Various procedures for requiring the other side to provide information during a case in court. Examples are interrogatories, depositions, and requests for admissions.

docket. The cases that have been filed at a specific court.

docket number. The number the clerk's office assigns to a specific case. This number is used to track the case and thus, it must be placed on each court paper.

domestic violence. Violence or threats of violence between spouses, former spouses, people living together or who formerly lived together, or people who have or had an intimate relationship.

equitable division. The standard for dividing marital property in New Hampshire based on "fairness." The law assumes that a 50/50 division is fair in most cases.

evidentiary hearing. A hearing with one or more witnesses giving testimony.

ex-parte. Emergency orders, issued without advance notice or the court hearing from both sides.

Family Division. The court that handles divorce and other family law cases.

fault divorce. A divorce based on the bad conduct (adultery, cruelty, drunkenness, etc.) of one spouse. About one percent of divorces are based on fault.

final hearing. The hearing that hears the evidence and rules on the divorce, the grounds for divorce, the property division, and other provisions.

final order. The order or decree that includes the divorce, the grounds for divorce, the property division, and other provisions.

financial affidavit. Required court form in divorce and parenting cases. Includes income and asset information.

first appearance. The first court event in a divorce or parenting case. The judge or master talks to a group of couples about the court process, and how to settle the issues without litigation. At this event, the court refers many cases to mediation.

four-way. In Collaborative Practice, a meeting of the two lawyers and two clients to resolve the issues in the case.

grounds. The legal basis for a divorce. Most New Hampshire divorces are no-fault (irreconcilable differences), but adultery, cruelty, and other fault grounds are available.

guardian *ad litem* (GAL). A person appointed by the court to represent the best interests of a child or children in a divorce or parenting case.

guidelines. The formula for calculating child support in New Hampshire. With certain exceptions, the resulting figure is the amount of support that must be paid.

hearing. A court event to make decisions about one or more of the divorce issues or a dispute about the procedure. The parties and lawyers are required to attend.

hearing notice. Document issued by clerk's office that shows date, time, location, and topic of court hearing or conference. May include the length of time allotted, instructions on what to bring to the hearing, or the procedures that will be used at the hearing.

interrogatories. A type of discovery consisting of formal written questions that must be answered under oath.

irreconcilable differences. A ground for divorce not based on the fault of either spouse (also called "no-fault").

irremediable breakdown. When one spouse refuses to continue the marriage and circumstances make it clear no change of heart is possible.

joint decision-making. Parents share the right to make

major decisions for their child and both have access to school and medical records.

joint petition. A request for divorce filed jointly by both spouses. This can be done when they agree on the need for divorce, the reasons (grounds) for divorce, and the basic facts about the family.

judge. A judicial officer appointed by New Hampshire's governor and executive council. Judges hear various types of cases, including divorce cases.

law clerk. Law student or law school graduate who is not yet a lawyer. Assists a lawyer or judge.

lawyer. Person licensed by the New Hampshire Supreme Court to give legal advice and represent clients in court.

litigation. A method of resolving legal disputes by the master or judge making the decisions.

mandatory retirement. Payroll deduction for certain retirement plans, generally those for government employees; it is used in the calculation of child support.

marital property. Assets to be divided in a divorce or legal separation. In New Hampshire, all assets in joint names or in the name of either the husband or the wife are marital property.

master (also **marital master**). A judicial officer appointed by the Judicial Branch to hear and decide divorce and other family law cases. Masters are full-time state employees.

mediation. A method of resolving disputes, in which a trained, neutral person helps the parties work out the solution for themselves.

mediated agreement. A divorce agreement, stipulation, or parenting plan worked out in mediation.

mediation-friendly lawyer. A lawyer who supports clients who choose this decision-making method.

memorandum of understanding. A mediated agreement.

motion. Court paper filed during the case seeking a specific order from the court.

motion hearing. A hearing on one or more motions. May be by offers of proof or by testimony.

need and ability to pay. The legal test used by the court when alimony is requested. It balances the financial need of the person seeking alimony against the other person's financial ability to pay alimony.

negotiation. A method of resolving legal disputes in which the parties' lawyers prepare and exchange a series of proposals. The proposals may be oral or written.

neutral evaluation. A court-sponsored program of alternate dispute resolution. The neutral (a volunteer lawyer) assists the parties and their lawyers in reaching an agreement, and may give an independent view of the likely outcome of a contested hearing. Some lawyers also offer such services as part of their private practice.

no-fault divorce. A divorce based on the breakdown of the marriage, without blame to either spouse. Approximately 99 percent of New Hampshire divorces are no-fault.

objection. A court paper filed to reply to a motion. Must be filed within ten days after the motion. This is also what a lawyer says during a trial, if the lawyer believes a question posed to a witness is improper.

offers of proof. A method of conducting temporary and some other hearings. Only the lawyers speak. Each lawyer summarizes the facts of the client's case and argues why the client's requests should be granted.

oath. A swearing to tell the truth.

order. Court paper issued by a clerk's office, containing either rulings on procedure or the court's decision on some or all issues. When the court approves an agreement of the parties, the agreement becomes a court order.

order of notice. Order issued at the beginning of a case, containing information on service, restraining order, the automatic restraining order on assets, and any *ex parte* orders.

parental rights and responsibilities. All rights and responsibilities parents have concerning their child.

parenting coordination. An ADR method of helping parents implement their parenting plan by improving communication and resolving disputes.

parenting plan. A written plan describing each parent's rights and responsibilities.

parenting schedule. The schedule of when the child is in the care of each parent.

partial agreement. A temporary or final agreement to some, but not all, of the pending issues. The judge or master decides the issues that are not agreed upon.

parties. The people officially a part of a divorce or other lawsuit; for example, the husband and wife in a divorce.

perjury. The crime of lying under oath.

petition. New Hampshire court papers filed to start a divorce, after-divorce, unwed, or other family law case.

petitioner. A person who files a petition. If a couple files a joint petition, the person whose name is listed first in the case name is the petitioner.

plan administrator. The person legally responsible for a retirement plan; this person deals with QDROs.

premarital or prenuptial agreement. Agreement prior

to marriage or civil union as to what would happen if the couple divorces or if one spouse dies. The agreement usually concerns property; sometimes alimony is part of the agreement.

pretrial conference. A court conference to plan for the final contested hearing.

pro bono. A program of the New Hampshire Bar Association that provides free representation to clients who meet strict financial guidelines.

proposed order. Each side's request to the court containing the order he or she would like granted.

pro se. A person representing him or herself in a court case.

property. Assets, including real property (real estate), furniture and other house contents, vehicles, bank accounts, retirement accounts.

QDRO (Qualified Domestic Relations Order). An order to divide retirement benefits.

QMCSO (Qualified Medical Child Support Order). An order concerning health insurance for a child.

referee. A judicial officer who decides cases when the only issue is child support.

return date. The deadline for filing an appearance.

residential responsibility. A parent's responsibility to provide a home for the child.

respondent. A person who receives court papers in a divorce or other family law case. If a couple files a joint petition, the person whose name is listed second in the case name is the respondent.

restraining order. An order not to do a specific thing; for example, not to take the child out of New England or not to enter the other spouse's home.

rules. The court procedures for a particular type of case. The Family Division has rules for divorce and other family cases.

second opinion. Review, by another lawyer, of your case and representation to date.

service. The procedure of the sheriff delivering a petition (or motion) to a respondent or other party. It is sufficient that the sheriff leaves the papers at the person's residence unless there are *ex parte* orders. By arrangement, service may be accepted at the sheriff's office.

settlement conference. A court conference to consider whether or not the case can be settled.

split parenting. Each of the parents has one or more of the children living with him or her most of the time.

standing order (SO). Part of the uniform support order. The SO contains basic legal terms that apply to all cases, unless the uniform support order makes an exception.

status conference. A court conference to review how a case is progressing.

stipulation. An agreement filed to resolve some or all of the issues in a divorce or other case.

scheduling conference. A court conference, to schedule the steps required to complete the case. Occurs at the beginning of a case without minor children.

subpoena. A document requiring a person to attend a hearing or deposition; it may also require that he or she bring certain items.

Supreme Court. The highest court in the New Hampshire state court system. Hears appeals from lower state courts and administrative agencies.

temporary agreement or order. Sets out the terms that will be in place until the final agreement or order takes effect.

temporary hearing. A court hearing to resolve the short-term issues in a case. It results in a temporary order that specifies each party's rights and responsibilities while the case is ongoing.

term. One provision in an agreement or order. Deals with a specific issue.

testimony. At a hearing or deposition, what a witness says under oath in response to direct and cross-examination.

uncontested divorce. All issues have been resolved between the parties or by mediation, or by negotiation. Whether a divorce is uncontested cannot be known until the end of the case.

uniform support order (USO). A court form required if there is a minor child. It summarizes the order on child support, alimony (if any), health insurance, and uninsured health costs. If there is an agreement on these issues, the parties sign and file a USO.

waive. Give up a right.

∞

index

Index

Amoskeag Press

P.O. Box 33
TEMPLE, NH 03084

The New Hampshire Divorce Handbook
is available at your local bookstore or
direct from the publisher.

~

*To order from Amoskeag Press, send
this coupon (or a copy) with a
check or money order, or see
www.amoskeagpress.com.*

Name _____

Address _____

City

State _____ Zip_____

Please send me _____ copies. Total enclosed $_____

Total cost; includes regular shipping and handling*:

Quantity	Price per book	Shipping & Handling	Total Cost*
1 book	$24	$6	$30
2 books	$24	$6	$54
3 books	$20	$7	$67

**Add $4 per order for priority mail service to NH/MA
Contact us about prices and fees for larger quantities.*

About the Author

ATTORNEY HONEY HASTINGS opened her law practice in Hillsborough County, New Hampshire in 1982. In 1983, she co-founded the Family Law Section of the New Hampshire Bar Association. More recently, Hastings co-founded the Collaborative Law Alliance of New Hampshire, and has served as its president.

Her practice has embraced many aspects of family law: divorce, legal separation, post-divorce, parenting (custody), child support/alimony, property division (including retirement benefits), unwed families, paternity, grandparents' rights, interstate/international child abduction, interstate family disputes, premarital agreements, adoption, guardianships of minors, and family law appellate work.

Since 2005, Ms. Hastings has restricted her practice to helping people resolve conflicts using collaborative practice, mediation, unbundled legal services, and parenting coordination. She no longer handles litigated divorces or parenting cases, but advises people in these situations. She has also been called as an expert witness in lawyer discipline and malpractice cases.

She is a member of the New Hampshire Conflict Resolution Association, and is an Advanced Practitioner in Family Mediation of the Association for Conflict Resolution. She received her JD in 1980 from Boston College Law School and her BA from Lincoln University in Pennsylvania in 1967. After graduation from law school, she drafted bills for the New Hampshire Legislature. She is admitted to the bars of New Hampshire, the Federal District Court of New Hampshire, the First Circuit Court of Appeals, and the Supreme Court of the United States.

Ms. Hastings writes about family law topics for lay people, lawyers, mediators, and mental health professionals, using the "plain language" that has been a hallmark of her practice. Her articles have appeared in various American Bar Association and New Hampshire Bar Association publications. The first edition of the *New Hampshire Divorce Handbook* was published in 1999. She speaks on family law issues, to both lay and professional audiences, on topics such as parental rights and responsibilities, retirement plans, child support laws, bankruptcy and divorce. Through Amoskeag Continuing Education, she presents continuing education programs approved for lawyers, mediators, and mental health professionals.

Attorney Hastings is an avid gardener, conservationist, and participant in town government.

Keep up with Changes
in Family Law!

The New Hampshire Legislature regularly makes
changes in the laws on divorce and other family issues. The
Family Division changes divorce procedures. New Hampshire
Supreme Court decisions interpret the law.

To learn how these changes might effect the information in
this book and thus your divorce, please check
www.NHDivorceHandbook.com.